Anchored

fifty devotions to encourage and inspire

Anchored: fifty devotions to encourage and inspire
Published (2015) by Village Creek Bible Camp

All individual contributors maintain individual ownership and rights to their written and art contributions published in this book. Each has granted permission for printing of these materials in this collection.

ISBN: 1512190136
ISBN-13: 978-1512190137

Compiled and edited by Stacy A. Bender
Cover art and design by Lori R. Hetteen – Used with permission

Editor's Acknowledgements

We give all honor and glory to God, our Creator, Redeemer, and Sustainer. From the first seed being planted in March, 2015, to publication in May, 2015, God has gifted, guided, and given favor. All praise be to Him for this project!

My husband and kids (Elizabeth and Josiah) have been valuable sounding boards, critical eyes, and encouragers through this entire process. Thank you!

Lori Hetteen provided the cover art and was a sounding board for most things related to layout, design, and art. She shares her heart about this theme and gives us insight into how she created the cover art after the introduction to the book. More information about Lori and where to find her artwork can be found at the end of the book. Thank you!

Sue Lyford provided all of the business-related support as well as the Village Creek Bible Camp portions of the marketing through Facebook, Twitter, and mass emails. Thank you!

Anita Pelzer provided critical editing eyes - a "last catch" for all of those tricky punctuation and grammar issues. Thank you!

Tom and Camie Treptau, as executive director and co-director of Village Creek Bible Camp, provided initial approval of, direction for, and support throughout the project. Thank you!

Over 40 people, ranging in age from late teens to octogenarians, have contributed to this project. Each person involved and his or her particular contribution and gifting, entirely donated and without personal gain, has made this book become a reality. Readers can find information about individual authors at the end of the book. Thank you to each author!

All net proceeds from this project will go to support the ministries at Village Creek Bible Camp (VCBC) located in Lansing, Iowa. The camp provides year-round camps, retreats, and other programming for all ages.

More information about VCBC is available at the end of this book.

If you use this devotion over the summer, consider using the prayer guide on page 125 to pray for VCBC or another Christian camp – perhaps one that you support or live near.

Introduction

I sat across from Camie Treptau, co-director of Village Creek Bible Camp located in Lansing, Iowa, at breakfast. We have known each other for over a decade, and – typical in ministry circles – we always pick up right where we left off whenever we see each other. We had updated each other on our lives and had laughed quite a bit.

I watched Camie's face change from the smile associated with the laughter we had experienced to disbelief, to excitement, and then to fear as I said, "I have a crazy idea, Camie. Let's do a devotion book with authors who are tied to Village Creek, with a theme that is the summer theme, and with the proceeds supporting camp. Let's do it for this year – let's publish it before summer camp season starts!"

What seemed to be an overwhelming project at the time of that initial conversation is now in your hands.

Although the inspiration for the theme of this book comes from the specific theme at a specific Bible camp during a specific summer, its truths apply to the lives of any believer, anywhere, and at just about any time.

God is our anchor through all of our present life as well as in the eternal life that we are promised. When we acknowledge our need for a Savior, recognize that Christ provided forgiveness for our sins through His death and resurrection, and choose to follow Him, we grab onto an anchor. From that moment, God is an anchor who is with us and for us in our present and for eternity.

The prayer of all involved in this project is that the book will find its way into the hands of anyone who needs or desires inspiration, challenge, and encouragement in their relationship with God through Jesus Christ.

-sb, editor

About the Cover Art

Hebrews 6:19 (NASB)
*This hope we have as an anchor of the soul,
a hope both sure and steadfast and one which enters within the veil.*

Life is wonderful. But it is often a mess. Whether it is actually falling apart as terribly as we perceive it to be or we are only being a bit dramatic, things do not usually look exactly as we would like them to. Relationships are difficult, jobs are not fulfilling, children get sick, there are horrific natural disasters, and people are just plain jerks to each other. If you are currently breathing, you know it's rough.

It is no secret, least of all to the creator of the world, that we have mucked things up. We chose ourselves over Him and over one another. God had a plan to fix that. He became flesh and descended to earth as Jesus who took our sins, paid the penalty for them, killed death, and sat down next to his Father, his job finished once and for all time. As the perfect sacrifice, Jesus was able to enter into the presence of God, the holy of holies, within the veil. And according to the writer of Hebrews, that is where we are held – right there in the same space as God Almighty. We are anchored there, with the one who made us, knows us, and sees our needs better than we do.

God, being the author of our life and the embodiment of love, did not and does not leave us experiencing our troubles alone. His Spirit dwells in us and there is no place we go that is cut off from Him. We could find ourselves in the middle of the sea, on the far side of the sea, or completely covered by the sea, and our anchor would remain. Our God is not content to watch us flailing from the shore. He is the kind of God who walks out on the crashing waves to meet us where we are. He is with us. He is for us.

It would do us good to remember there is a whole plan unfolding here on this planet. There is life happening outside of our individual messes. In fact, there is life happening right there in middle of our messes. God does not waste things. He is willing and able to use all circumstances for His glory and our good.

The mystery of God and His activity is that He has worked in the past, He is working the present, and He will work in the future. He has made all things new. He is making all things new. And He will make all things new in the future.

As we trust and obey the only one who is worthy, we are able to see that we are held and that God has a life abundant with his beauty for us to live.

These are truths that were kicking around in my head as I drew the cover art for this book. It is my prayer for each one of us that we would endeavor to know the One who has made us, that we would understand just a tiny portion of His affections for us, and that we would use the skills He has given us to love others and bring Him praise.

Author/Artist: Lori Hetteen

We have an anchor that keeps the soul
Steadfast and sure while the billows roll,
Fastened to the Rock which cannot move,
Grounded firm and deep in the Savior's love.[i]

PRISCILLA J. OWENS

From the Beginning

Genesis 1:1-2 (ESV)

In the beginning, God created the heavens and the earth.
The earth was without form and void,
and darkness was over the face of the deep.
And the Spirit of God was hovering over the face of the waters.

The opening words of Genesis are some of the most beautiful, not only in Scripture, but in all literature. There is something dark and brooding – a world covered in darkness and the chaos of a churning ocean. A world that is uninhabited and uninhabitable hanging in the center of a dark and inhospitable universe. And hovering over the chaos of the churning waters – a supernatural presence – the very presence of the Creator, the Spirit of God.

And with the sound of His voice, the universe is forever changed:

- O Out of chaos – ORDER!.
- O Out of darkness – LIGHT!
- O Out of the void – LIFE!

That which was uninhabited and uninhabitable is now teeming with life. That which was covered in darkness is now illuminated in light. That which was void and meaningless has order and purpose.

I fear that too often I forget that the one who is my anchor also hovers over the chaotic storms of my life. I forget that Christianity is not primarily about holding on in the storm but about trusting enough to set sail. I need to recognize that the voice of God calls out to me in the chaos, the darkness, and the void and provides order, light, and life.

I fear that we too often view this life as something to be endured, something to survive, or something to "weather." Therefore, we forget that God is more than just an anchor – make no mistake about it – HE IS AN ANCHOR! And I thank God that He is there! But His presence, His company, His Spirit is also constantly hovering in the midst of our lives providing order, light, and life.

And this is not just any order, but an order that gives purpose to each of us – to bear His very image to a world that needs to see Him. Not just any light, but the light that shines before all humanity. Not just any life, but the abundant life that comes from following Jesus Christ!

Father God: thank you for being my anchor in the times of storm, and thank you for your presence that hovers over the waters of life calling us to set sail with lives of order, light, and life.

Author: Kerry L. Bender

I Love Sitting by the Creek!

Matthew 7:24-25 (ERV)

Whoever hears these teachings of mine and obeys them is like a wise man who built his house on rock. It rained hard, the floods came, and the winds blew and beat against that house. But it did not fall because it was built on rock.

I have loved sitting by the creek that runs through Village Creek Bible Camp since the first summer I attended as a camper in fifth grade. Since the time that I first attended back then, the creek bank has moved. The distance from where I sat on the bench back then in comparison to where I sit now looking down into the creek is quite dramatic. For my daughter's school project, my husband and co-director of the camp even did a Google search and found older maps of the area.

The creek bank has actually shifted all throughout the property of the camp.

We have witnessed a couple of times when the creek waters start to rise and actually to flood a good portion of the camp. These events have taken out an archery target and a shed. The force of the water is amazing to observe as it brings down trees, transports debris, and moves lots of mud.

There is one spot in camp, though, that has not moved in the last 10 years because, in anticipation of frequent floods, we finally helped anchor it with very large rocks. A big bulldozer dropped in large rocks, some that are heavier than a person. It now provides an anchor not only for that whole section of the creek but also for a good portion of the creek further around its original impact area.

That is the thing with anchors; they help hold things securely in place while also providing support to areas around it. I love that! I love that anchors provide security when storms or doubts come. Jesus openly taught that we need to be building on a firm foundation. And, throughout God's Word, He shares with us the very truth about on what – upon whom – it is that we should anchor our life.

These are just a few of the truths that I am anchored to:

1. God loves me and sent His son to make a way for me to have a relationship with Him (John 3:16)
2. He created me for a purpose and a plan – I'm not a mistake (Ephesians 2:10, and Psalm 139)
3. And as His child, when the storms of life come He will be with me (Isaiah 43:2-3)
4. I need to get into His Word, the Bible, often so that I can counter the lies of the evil one (John 10:10)

There are so many more. Go dig in, and find some great truths that encourage you. God, as our anchor, desires for us to be in relationship with Him so that He can provide the solid ground for our lives here on earth and into eternity. My relationship with Jesus truly is my anchor.

Father God: Be with us, call to us in the storm, and help us to build our life on the foundation that we can find in you for today and for eternity.

Author: Camie Treptau

Remember

Joshua 4:20-24 (NIV)

And Joshua set up at Gilgal the twelve stones they had taken out of the Jordan. He said to the Israelites, "In the future when your descendants ask their parents, 'What do these stones mean?' tell them, 'Israel crossed the Jordan on dry ground. For the LORD your God dried up the Jordan before you until you had crossed over...He did this so that all the peoples of the earth might know that the hand of the LORD is powerful and so that you might always fear the LORD your God."

A few years ago my husband and I, along with our three kids and his parents (yep, 7 of us in a minivan), drove to Colorado via the Black Hills. It was nearly dinner time and we were still an hour or so from our destination with nothing in sight. I realized sitting in the car that we probably were not going to see the one thing I had been dreaming of since the AAA lady marked it on our Triptik...the Oregon Trail ruts. Yes, you might laugh but after years of playing Oregon Trail on the computer and more years of teaching junior high and high school kids about westward migration I really wanted to see them. Then something amazing happened. As the kids were asking, yet again, when we were going to eat my husband took the exit and we drove about 15 miles to the spot.

The stone in that area is soft, and the endless numbers of wagons on the trail created ruts in the rock that are 6 feet deep in some places. Even the hungry children were amazed that we could still see evidence of anxious settlers rumbling through Nebraska and Wyoming on their way west over 150 years ago. It's an incredible reminder of their effort as you look for miles and see nothing and feel the hot sun.

As we zip down the interstate at 75 mph we forget that it wasn't too long ago it took months, not hours, to travel west. We forget that our lives are easier because of someone else's sacrifice. So much of life is like that. How often do I forget the small, good things, even a day or two later...much less years later. God knows this about us and He wanted the Israelites to be reminded of His faithfulness.

What stands out most to me in these verses is that Joshua uses the word "you." The Lord your God dried up the Jordan before "you.". Parents 150 years after the stones were placed were supposed to say to their children, "God did this for you, for us, not just for them. He did this so that His glory and power would be evident to ALL for ALL time!"

I'm glad we stopped and saw those ruts. I'm glad my kids got a glimpse into the long, hot days on the trail. It gives them perspective. Those stones by the Jordan give perspective too. As Christians we are anchored to the past. But that anchor doesn't hold us back. Rather, we are held steady as we move forward by the faithfulness of God, not just to us, but to generations of His people. God's faithfulness in the past makes a way for us to move forward into the future He has for us!

Dear Father, as the busyness of life presses in, help me to remember that you are faithful in all things. Small things. Big things. Everything. And when I can't see how things will turn out, when the waters seem too scary, remind me again of your faithfulness to me. Amen.

Author: Jen Woyke

Henna in High-Rises

1 Peter 2:11-12 (NLT)

Dear friends, I warn you as "temporary residents and foreigners" to keep away from worldly desires that wage war against your very souls. Be careful to live properly among your unbelieving neighbors. Then even if they accuse you of doing wrong, they will see your honorable behavior, and they will give honor to God when he judges the world.

Most days my life is pretty tame. I don a suit, sensible shoes, and sit in an office. I'm a lawyer who spends most of my days doing tedious, detail-oriented tasks. The hours tick by as I measure my time in 6-minute increments.

But I had a chance to break up this routine and have an adventure: I went to a rural province in India to volunteer at an orphanage for HIV-positive orphans. The trip was everything I expected--weird food, amazing kids, and perpetual reminders that I have too much stuff. The trip went by in a flash. Before we knew it, we began our 27-hour journey home. Just before dashing to the airport, we squeezed in time to get henna.

Henna is a reddish-brown paste that people in India use to make beautiful temporary designs on skin. It is like a temporary tattoo but with loads of intricate geometric designs that wrap around your hands and fingers up to your elbow. You temporarily become a walking piece of art, broadcasting to the world that you traveled to some exotic locale.

So, I returned home, henna-marked. And life continued. But this time, everywhere I went people knew something was different. At first, I felt embarrassed and wondered what my coworkers would think. It was clear that I had been somewhere beyond the confines of my cushy office.

As each person noticed the marks, they asked about the trip. Each time felt like a chance, an opportunity to share about a God who deeply cared for HIV-positive kiddos in rural India *and* for over-worked twenty-somethings.

But as the henna prompted their questions, it made me wonder: why did it take a temporary tattoo from around the world for my coworkers to realize there was something different about me, that I originated from another place? We, as followers of Christ are called to be different—to be strangers or foreigners on the earth. It should be apparent that we know our home is not in this life.

So when we speak, our language should be foreign, beautiful, and seasoned with grace. When we act it should be according to the love of the One whose love knows no bounds. And when we think, our thoughts should be informed with the wisdom that comes from knowing that it is God who is in control of all things.

God: May our actions and deeds point to you. When we walk through life, may our steps be so different from what is expected that people will want to know the cause for actions. Give us humility and courage to share who our Originator is. Amen.

Author: Bri Turner

You are More Valuable

Matthew 6:26 (ESV)

Look at the birds of the air;
they do not sow or reap or store away in barns,
and yet your heavenly Father feeds them.
Are you not much more valuable than they?

I recently watched a PBS special[ii] about how a tiny songbird, that weighs no more than two tablespoons of sugar (12 grams), accomplishes an amazing feat. Each fall, blackpoll warblers gather on the east shore of Canada and the United States and then migrate to Mexico. Atlantic fishermen reported finding the songbirds landing on their boats during storms. Some scientists were skeptical; such small birds certainly would not fly out over the ocean.

Would they not take the much safer route down along the coast? In 2013, a group of ornithologists set out to find out for sure. They placed small tracking devices on 40 of the song birds. In 2014, five of those birds were recaptured, the data was analyzed, and what they found was astonishing.

The songbirds flew some 1,700 miles in non-stop flights ranging from 49 to 73 hours, and almost all of the flights were over the ocean.

God has marvelously made these little creatures for this spectacular adventure. He also provides the miniscule insects they consume for the thousands of calories that will be burned on their trip

As I read the story of these incredible birds, I could not help but think of Jesus' instruction in the Sermon on the Mount to look at the birds and be reminded of God's love and care. And then His encouragement, that if God cares for tiny birds, how much more will He care for you – who are *"much more valuable."*

God doesn't always call us to take the safe or the easy route. Sometimes God asks us to take the route out over the ocean.

You may right now be in the midst of a 1,700 mile non-stop flight over the water, but be encouraged God has not forgotten you. He is able to sustain you, and will anchor you in His love and care.

The next time you see a bird fly by, pause and thank God for the wonderful reminder that He is able provide for them – and you!

God, thank you for promising to care for the creatures of your world, and for reminding me how valuable I am to you as well. Increase my faith to really trust you through this season of my life.

Author: Dan Andrews

When darkness seems to hide His face,
I rest on His unchanging grace.
In every high and stormy gale,
My anchor holds within the veil.[iii]

EDWARD MOTE

Loving the Love of God

Mark 12:30-31 (ESV)

And you shall love the Lord your God with all your heart and with all your soul and with all your mind and with all your strength. The second is this: you shall love your neighbor as yourself. There is no other commandment greater than these.

A few years ago the Lord shared something with me; it came amidst a season of being heavily involved in ministry. Little did I know that, while it was powerful at the time, it has become even more profound as I continue to live a life of following Jesus.

As a teenager, in the quiet of my room, I felt the Lord say, *"Courtney, I want you to love being my child more than you love being a leader for my people."*

I am slowly understanding what this means for my life. God wants me – the person, the relationship - more than He wants the things that I do for Him. This goes for all of us. God wants you to love being a child of His more than you love leading a Bible study, attending a small group, or even serving at a Bible camp. If you are thinking to yourself right now, 'I don't do any of those things', then you are in the prime spot to truly understand this best.

Many people summarize the greatest commandment as "love God, love others" - pretty simple, right? I think that sometimes living a life of ministry can cause us to focus more on the "loving others" part. I will even go so far as to say focusing on that above the "loving God" part. Maybe what would bring refreshment to your spirit is just sitting before God and meditating on His love for you.

Why is this crucial? Friends, it becomes easy to hide behind our works that we do for God; ministry can easily become an event that we put on our calendar. It might even be our occupation. Does He love it when we serve Him? Absolutely! But do we not realize that He wants us? The God of the universe wants *you!* Jesus wants the broken, beautiful, overwhelmed, hurting, thriving, anxious, raw and real you.

To love God is to know God, to abide in His Word, and to follow His lead. Is loving God vulnerable? It can be; standing before a holy God with the greatest commandment being to love Him - that sounds like quite a task. The beautiful thing is that Jesus is our example and He loved us first. He loves us because He loves us. If you need to reread that last sentence, we'll do it together.

Lord Jesus, help me to slow down and receive the perfect love that you have for me. Help me, by your Spirit, to understand that you want me more than you want the things I do for you. Thank you that loving you is what you require of me; teach me what that looks like for my life. O, the magnificence of your love! All of this I pray in Jesus Name. Amen.

Author: Courtney Aronson

Sheltered in the Shadows

Psalm 91:1 (ESV)
*He who dwells in the shelter of the Most High
will abide in the shadow of the Almighty.*

Because my parents divorced when I was quite young, I started travelling from North Dakota to the east coast at an early age. Every summer, kind aunts spent weeks taking me to the ocean, and I fell in love. Something in my soul responds to the sea. I love its sounds, its smells, and its gritty feel on my skin.

On a recent visit, I returned to a favorite beach north of Boston but went to a new part of the beach itself. Since a young age, I have loved to climb the rocks along the ocean, but I had not climbed these particular ones before. The emerald green that radiated from them drew me in. I wanted to see the life around them, near them, and under them.

As I climbed, I peered under the rocks and found life in the shadows. The rocks hid an entirely different world that teemed with all sorts of life. Snails, barnacles, seaweed, and little swimming thingees crawled, floated, and engaged with the tide while remaining completely safe there in the shadows.

I stayed for a while, climbed to higher ground to avoid getting my phone wet as the tide came in, and sat for a while to think, ponder, and wonder at this serene yet dangerous little spot that I had found.

When I think of being "safely under God's shadow," I connect that concept with inactivity, rest, and personal growth. However, the world that I observed in the shadows of the rocks along the coast revealed a different thought to me.

The safety of God's shadow does not remove us from life but rather provides His presence there in the midst of it all. God's shadow provides safety, care, and guidance while I continue to live life. He allows the winds and the waves to come my way; life is full of constant change, circumstances, and situations that often seem hazardous to us. Being in God's shadow will not always shield us from what can happen in a world filled with sin and sinful people.

However, regardless of how life happens around me, the truth is that I am safely under God's shadow as the winds blow, securely in His care as the big waves crash around me, and steadily able to do all He calls me to do. The truth is that I am in His care, His shadow, and His gaze at all times. His presence is with me. When I recognize this, I can choose to live in the peace, calm, and joy that is God.

What I feel, what I experience, and what I encounter cannot change the fact that God provides presence, safety, and redemption in His shadow. Like the emerald green life under the rocks along the coast that drew me to them, I can live abundantly because God provides His protective shadow.

Heavenly Father: thank you for your shadow of safety, security, calm, and peace. Help us to live in the truth of your care regardless of the winds and waves that try to pull us from believing the truth. Thank you for your shadow of safety.

Author: Stacy Bender

Quench Your Thirst

John 4:13-14 (NIV)

Jesus answered, "Everyone who drinks this water will be thirsty again, but whoever drinks the water I give them will never thirst. Indeed, the water I give them will become in them a spring of water welling up to eternal life."

When I was in eighth grade, my soccer team made it all the way to the state championship game. That day in Indianapolis was blazing hot. I remember vividly how incredibly thirsty I was during that game. My mouth and throat were so dry and parched. Every time I came off the field, I gulped water like crazy.

Athletes know that after any hard practice, workout, or race, we get incredibly thirsty. Water refreshes us and quenches our thirst like nothing else. Water is essential to our ability to perform at a very high level. I have heard that we should drink half of our weight in ounces of water - everyday. That is a lot of water – everyday.

We are also spiritually thirsty. I do not have to look very hard to see a lack of love, bad moral behavior, anger, chaos and evil in our world. Some may give all kinds of reasons as to why, but I believe it is because we are spiritually thirsty. You and I crave something that only Christ can give us.

Jesus tells us this in today's verses. The living water He is talking about is real, and it is found in a relationship with Christ.

Just like our bodies physically crave water to sustain us, our souls crave to be filled by something that is Real and Eternal.

Would you be willing to drink of this "living water" Jesus is talking about?

Dear Jesus I admit there are times I am so thirsty for you. I need the living water you talk about. I want it. My soul longs for it. I know I will find it through a relationship with you Jesus. I love you Jesus.

Author: Jake Vanada

Rooted

Jeremiah 17:7-8 (NIV)

But blessed is the one who trusts in the LORD, whose confidence is in him. They will be like a tree planted by the water that sends out its roots by the stream. It does not fear when heat comes; its leaves are always green. It has no worries in a year of drought and never fails to bear fruit.

No one ever likes being picked on at school, at work, wherever. For me, elementary school wasn't the best. When I switched schools for junior high, I decided to make all NEW friends and be in the popular crowd. I didn't change who I was, but I just decided to fit in like a chameleon and follow along. I had the biggest and best swimming/sleepover party for my birthday and thought everything was great. However, when summer came, I realized that none of those "friends" really called me anymore. I wondered if they were really true friends at all.

That summer, our family decided to fly to Florida for a vacation. We are not talking a commercial airliner but a small 6-seater single engine plane piloted by my dad. We had a great time until on the way home. We flew right into a thunderstorm. The plane was shaking just like in the old movies; we could see lightning out the windows and rain on the windshield. It was like the most incredible roller coaster ride ever, but we were dropping hundreds of feet at a time. The turbulence was so loud in the plane that I started singing a popular Christian song at the top of my lungs, and no one could hear me. The lyrics by Annie Herring were, "If this were the last day of my life, I would not cry, for I've been waiting for it."

It was so weird – I was smiling when I really should have been scared! But I was anchored, rooted, with nothing to fear. When we came out of the storm, it was as if our plane was in a sideways pocket of clouds with the sunset waiting at the opening. It was incredible, and I'll never forget it!

A few days later, I came to Village Creek Bible Camp for summer camp. I had come every year since 5th grade, so it was always a highlight. It was during that week that I made a life changing realization. In talking to the youth pastors and re-living that crazy plane ride, I realized that my NEW friends at school would have been terrified if they had been in my place. I was the one who was not the "true" friend.

I had the answers and was anchored in Christ, yet I hadn't been willing to share that with my friends at school as I was too busy trying to fit in. God loves all of my friends and wants me to introduce them to Him so that they can have the same hope and roots that I have.

Father God – Help me to put my trust and confidence in you, being well anchored or rooted, so that when the storms of life or drought comes, I have no fear or worries, and never fail to bear fruit.

Author: Gela Ashcroft

Desiring to Serve God

2 Timothy 1:7 (ESV)
God did not give us a spirit of timidity, but a Spirit of power.
James 4:17 (ESV)
*So whoever knows the right thing to do and fails to do it,
for him it is sin.*

Whenever God asks me to do something for Him, my initial reaction is almost always to say no and then to come up with excuses to justify my reluctance. My second reaction and realization is generally to remember what God taught me over a year ago: that He would never ask me to do anything for Him that He would not be with me through.

My unwillingness to serve comes from a place of weakness, for I struggle to believe that I can be of any real use to God. Although this may sound humble, it is far from it. It actually shows a lack of faith in God's ability to use me—in essence, it is me limiting God's power in my life. I realized that this wrong view of the power of God was holding me back from doing things for Him. I would not step out of my comfort zone and share my faith. I would not go on missions trips. I would not speak to groups about God because I lacked the faith that He would be there for me if things grew difficult for me.

My failure to act is a failure to trust God. It is a failure to do what He says, to be useful to Him, and to glorify Him.

These verses have taught me a solid lesson. I realized that, as a Christian, I am called to much more than avoidance of sin; I am called to action. God calls me to make a difference, to step out of my comfort zone, to be a light in the darkness, to preach the gospel in season and out, and to be a testimony to the One whose name I bear if I call myself a Christian. Because, if I am proud of being a Christian, I had better be Christ-like. If not, I am not representing Him.

I say all this as an encouragement, not only to you, but to myself as well. An encouragement to realize that God has grace enough for you regardless of where you are. However, His greatest calling for you is to live a life so sold out for Him that you never consider the difficulties of following Him. That is not an easy calling; it is not something that will happen overnight. It is a process, and it takes time, dedication, and effort. However, the result is a life that honors and pleases God. That life will produce a better relationship with Him than you could ever imagine.

Heavenly Father: Give us faith in your ability to walk us through whatever you ask of us. Grant us opportunities to step out in faith for your glory.

Author: Jonathan Chavalas

How firm a foundation, ye saints of the Lord,
Is laid for your faith in His excellent Word!
What more can He say than to you He hath said,
You, who unto Jesus, for refuge have fled? [iv]

JOHN RIPPON

My Treasure

Psalm 119:11 (NASB)
*Your word I have treasured in my heart
that I might not sin against you.*

Getting ready for Bible camp is so fun. Just thinking and planning about what to put in my suitcase is such a joy. In my early years, my mom would sew me some new PJs and other things I wanted. And then of course I would buy some goodies. Each year, there were different clothes, shoes, tooth brush, or whatever.

But there was one thing that was always the same and something I knew always had to be there. *My Bible.*

Camp was filled with fun activities that were different each year. It seemed that camp leaders never lacked for new and exciting things to do. But there was something that was always the same, yet fresh and new – singing, praying, and listening to what God had to say to me. There were always times to be alone with God and treasure God's Word in my heart.

And then there were those wonderful counselors with just the right words at just the right time. I remember one of my first counselors in junior camp. I only remember two words that she said "Hello, Ramona." I am always called Monie but this time she used Ramona for a reason.

My girlfriend and I had just settled down to sleep when we heard a scratching on the screen. It was two boys asking us to meet them behind the cabin. We got up, snuck out, and were sure no one had heard us. We sat out behind the cabin and ate pretzels. It was kind of fun doing something we knew we should not.

Our very wise counselor did not come out and get us even though she knew where we were. She did something much wiser. She got in my bed.

After some time we snuck back in ever so quietly. Just as I was about to get into bed my counselor said, "Hello, Ramona!"

I about jumped out of my skin. She got up and went to her bed while I got into mine. Nothing was ever said the next day. I did not have to be reminded of the night before. I knew.

Camp was one of those places, away from the hustle and bustle of life, where I realized what a treasure the Bible really was. It taught me how to live. It kept me from sinning.

Your Word have I treasured in my heart, that I might not sin against you.

I never snuck out at night again. That boy who scratched on the screen continued to be my close friend for some years and has been my life partner for 60 years.

Father, your Word is such a treasure. It keeps us close to you. And you keep us from sin. We love you!

Author: Monie Fluth

High Weeds

Psalms 32:5 (ESV)
I acknowledged my sin to you,
and I did not cover my iniquity;
I said, "I will confess my transgressions to the Lord,"
and you forgave the iniquity of my sin. Selah

Recently, my family went on vacation to Florida to visit our extended families and spend some time at the beach. It was wonderful! Everything went about as close to perfect as one could hope.

Back home in Oklahoma, however, something else had been going on. Before we left on vacation, I mowed our lawn. However, I knew I needed to get someone to do it while we were gone. Two weeks away, and I would be coming home to a jungle.

I did not find someone before the trip. I forgot. My mind was already half way to Florida, and I messed up. Sure enough, as we pulled in to the drive, I could see the impressive height of my grass in the moonlight.

The next morning I pulled out my push mower, stared at my grass, and knew I was in for the great lawn battle of 2015. I was kicking myself for not getting things squared away before we left. I was frustrated and defeated before I even started. In fact, even though I pulled out my mower in the morning, I did not begin mowing until late afternoon. I convinced myself the grass was too wet to start (it was not) and found something else to do.

By the time I started actually cutting grass I only had and hour or so of daylight left. Sure enough, when my measly push mower met the two feet tall matts of Bermuda, it choked right out. I could have called for help. I have friends with lawn tractors. I could have called a lawn service. It would not have cost too much. But no, not me. I was content to stay mad and frustrated and to cut this grass by myself.

Then, like a man on a white horse, my next door neighbor emerged from his shed riding a zero turn John Deere lawn tractor. He heard me stall my little push mower more times than he could take. I had been saved!

I do this more times than I would like to admit. Not with the lawn, but with my life. There are times when I sin, I see the consequences, and I immediately start this battle in my head. I feel guilty and defeated, like there's no way God can still love me now.

But then, there's Jesus. Instead of me carrying the burden of my sin, Jesus is there just waiting for us to confess it to Him so He can carry it for us.

Too often we spend hours, days, months, and years dwelling on our past failures. But confession and repentance is the pathway for experiencing our freedom in Christ. We need not be anchored down by past mistakes for which Jesus has already paid the penalty. Instead, anchor yourself in the grace and forgiveness that He offers.

Father God, I confess…

Author: Randy Strickland

Guitars and Hurricanes

Proverbs 17:19 (NIV)
As water reflects the face, so one's life reflects the heart.

When moving to the coast, we thought we were trading tornados for hurricanes. No one mentioned that if conditions are right, some hurricanes *spawn* hundreds of tornados. That information is apparently for natives only.

Our first Florida hurricane was Isaac, Category 1. He arrived as a very low threat, with high rain activity, and "... improving conditions for tornados and wind events." (Later we can discuss meteorological use of "improving" to mean "Prepare for Oz").

When the tornado sirens wailed, I was home with our two teenagers and one borrowed from another family. There are no basements in Florida, so our safest spot was our 8x8 laundry room with a washer, dryer and freezer. The remaining three feet was where the four of us would wait out the storm.

As we are piling into the room, our son asked, "What about the router?!" I knew he was right. The router must be unplugged. However it was upstairs. So as a brave mom I said, "You're right ... go unplug it."

In that sentence, I am admitting two things: 1) I do not know what a router looks like. 2) I will not win mom of the year. Ever.

He ran upstairs and reappeared seconds later - with his

guitar. I tried desperately to remember what childhood book we had read to him that taught about the importance of bringing a guitar to a natural disaster.

He stated simply, "I thought we might want to sing."

The ridiculousness was mounting. I looked to his sister, our daughter, who had raided the freezer for ice cream and was climbing on top of the dryer. Surely she would explain the geometry of relative space verses volume inequities. She took one quick look at her brother and the guitar and said, "Dude. That's awesome!"

My frustration was short-lived as I realized they were both old enough to grasp the situation. They were not being cavalier. They could not control what happened, but they could focus on something other than fear. The reflections of their hearts were at peace.

Every one of us has our "go to" position. When life hits, we default to some behavior. We whine and worry. Or we pray, worship and yield. Sometimes it is a combination of them all. If our default is a poor choice, then the storm can take us under. But if our default mode is anchored in the Word of God and reflecting His face, then why not bring a guitar to a hurricane?

Sweet Jesus, these days can be scary. Fill me with so much of you that fear cannot find a place to hide in my heart. Cause my life to reflect a heart sold out only to you.

Author: Sharon Czerwinski

Whatever You Do!

Colossians 3:17 (NIV)

*And whatever you do, whether in word or deed,
do it all in the name of the Lord Jesus,
giving thanks to God the Father through Him.*

I remember that, as a kid, I wanted to be the President of The United States. I am what you would call a bit of a dreamer. Maybe you can relate?

I asked my two boys what they would like to be when they grow up, and they said a policeman and a "dinosaur digger."

What do you want to be when you grow up? Whether you are 16 or 60 - if you could do anything with the next chapter of your life, what would it be? Dream!

I have found that there is a sense in the Christian community that the highest calling of a Christian is to be in full-time ministry. It seems if you are not a pastor or a missionary, you are somehow a second-rate Christian.

I believe that to be a pastor or missionary is a high calling. However, it is not any higher or any more full-time than any other calling that God puts on our hearts.

I love the way today's verse phrases this with such a wide and sweeping brush, "And *whatever you do... do it all for Jesus.*" Whatever you do!

The gifts and talents you have been given were given to you for a reason by the God of the universe. Whatever it is that you do with those gifts and talents, do it for the glory of God.

The world is in desperate need of Christian doctors, teachers, contractors, psychologists, insurance salesmen, farmers, company presidents and everything in between. Chase the dreams that burn within your soul, and give the glory to God.

The only way this works is for followers of Jesus to embrace the fact that, no matter what our dreams and passions are, we are called to full-time ministry. We must consciously decide that, whatever we do or say, we will do it all in the name of Jesus, giving thanks to God through Him.

This must be the foundation to which we anchor ourselves as followers of Jesus. We must understand that we are living out our individual callings as a part of a much larger story that God has written. He wants us to participate in His story, but in order to allow this to happen, we must be willing to surrender our desire to steal His glory.

Holy God: help me to be all in for you. Allow me to step aside and let you do what you will in my life in whatever way you see fit. Call me, give me the courage to go, and be with me as I do.

Author: Austin Walker

Cut From the Rock

Isaiah 51:1 (NIV)

Listen to me, you who pursue righteousness and who seek the Lord; Look to the rock from which you were cut and to the quarry from which you were hewn;

During my years teaching at the high school and junior college level, I have met students of all ages who are in tough situations; events that left them asking, "How am I ever going to get through this? How will I survive this?"

It may be the loss of a job, a torn friendship, or a family crisis. These are the moments when we feel that we are drowning in deep, dark waters and there seems to be no way out. Sometimes we try to "fix" our problems with false securities or by ignoring them, pretending they don't exist, shoving them deep down to eventually raise their ugly heads again. They almost seems to enslave us.

Isaiah spoke to this when he said, "Consider the quarry from which you are cut..." He was speaking to the nation of Israel reminding them of who they are in God. He reminds them that Abraham and Sarah had waited for twenty-five years for a child. But God's promises for them came true. For through them the entire Jewish nation was born. We, as believers in Jesus Christ, have also been cut from the Rock of Ages – our Creator, the LORD Jesus Christ.

When we look at how God has worked in our past, we can

be assured that His promises are true and we can count on Him to be with us in our present and future situations. Scripture tells us that God's promises are more enduring than the stars.

In II Corinthians 4: 16-19, Paul writes, *"Therefore we do not lose heart. Though outwardly we are wasting away, yet inwardly we are being renewed day by day. For our light and momentary troubles are achieving for us an eternal glory that far outweighs them all. So we fix our eyes not on what is seen, but on what is unseen. For what is seen is temporary, but what is unseen is eternal."*

Keeping our focus on God and His future promises can give us a deep joy in the midst of great trials. It also frees us to begin to move forward when we realize there is hope in Christ. Hope in Christ is the one motivating factor even in the darkest of moments.

When you are struggling, do you remember "The Rock" from which you have been cut and the quarry where you were hewn? Live in freedom today as you focus on God and His great promises.

LORD, thank you for your promises; thank you for answered prayers in my past. Help me to be hopeful as I anticipate your future workings in my life and your return.

Author: Jane Kramer

When peace like a river attendeth my way,
When sorrows like sea billows roll;
Whatever my lot, Thou hast taught me to say,
"It is well, it is well with my soul!" [v]

HORATION SPAFFORD

Through the Ups and Downs

Psalm 25:5 (NIV)
Guide me in your truth and teach me,
for you are God my Savior, and my hope is in you all day long.

My heart rate accelerates with each step I take. I feel lightheaded. And slightly nauseous. Around me the crowd, which includes family members, is engaged in casual, cheerful conversation. The voices in my head are screaming in protest. *Don't you know what awaits us at the front of this line?*

They do. And they're thrilled. Eager anticipation motivates them forward. Dread weighs me down. *How did I ever let my kids talk me into a roller coaster ride… AGAIN!*

Before I can retreat, we are in the cars, secure in our seats. The roller coaster begins to move. It sounds rickety as the train of cars moves along the track. As it makes its ascent, it groans some, seeming to strain to pull its load uphill. The sound of people's excited chatter around me is muffled, drowned out by the barrage of anxious thoughts within.

I close my eyes. I swallow the bile that has risen into the back of my throat. Every muscle in my body is tensed in high-alert, preparing for the worst. And then… then… *oh no!* We plunge toward the ground, fast. Way too fast. Squeals of delight surround me, thankfully masking my own pathetic, fear-filled whimpers.

Before I can pass out, the ride is over.

"Wasn't it great, Mom?" my daughters cheer as we leave the coaster behind us. I nod feebly in agreement. I will myself to move forward with the group, walking on weak knees and wobbly legs.

I did it. I rode the coaster. And I am ok.

The truth is: Expert engineers, educated in and led by tried-and-true laws of physics, designed that roller coaster with great precision. And machinists, guided by those reliable designs, assembled the coaster with the utmost care and attention to detail – and double-, triple-checks, of course.

I do not like roller coaster rides. I do not expect to ever like them. But they taught me something about this ride that I live out daily called "faith."

In the ups and downs – the thrilling highs and agonizing lows – of moving through life with Christ, the truth is this: the God who engineered the universe did so with great precision. With the utmost care and attention to detail, Creator God formed my very being. As Psalm 25 continues, David tells me, *"The Lord is good and does what is right* (v. 8)... *The Lord leads with unfailing love* (v. 10)."

And so...when the Lord leads me into places I do not necessarily want to go, and when He takes me through circumstances I would not have chosen, do I trust Him completely?

Father God: I wait expectantly – with anticipation rather than dread – for the good things You will do in me and through me as I trust Your leading.

Author: Debbi Ladwig

The God Who is Greater Than Our Hearts

1 John 3:20 (ESV)
*...for whenever our heart condemns us,
God is greater than our heart, and he knows everything.*

Do you ever feel your heart condemn you? Does your heart ever feel wobbly and weak, while it seems those around you are strong and assured?

When the church vans started pulling up and the kids began piling out for the first week of junior camp, I wondered what on earth I'd gotten myself into.

What did a sinner and misfit like me have to offer these kids? Camp can be a place where everyone seems to have it together. Everyone's gathered for a common purpose. Everyone's on the same page of serving the Lord and pouring out God's love to the campers.

Maybe you are like I was during my days as a camp counselor. You find yourself in a gorgeous place, made by God—surrounded by beautiful people, gifted by God—and your heart is out of joint, condemning you of the sin within.

You may be wondering, "Do I really fit here?"

When our sin seems too much, when we don't seem to fit, we have an anchor in the God who is greater than our heart.

This God doesn't look at how you appear on the outside. He sees past the smiles and jokes. He sees inside, and He knows everything.

Will you look at Jesus: perfect for you, crucified for you, risen for you, and remember that this is the God who is greater than your sin, greater than your doubt, and greater than your heart?

Let your anchor sink deeply into this God, who knows it all and still calls you His own. In Christ, your sin is dead and there is no condemnation for you, not even from your own heart.

Father, thank you for being greater than our condemning hearts.

Author: Abigail Dodds

Who is the Star of the Story?

Daniel 1:17 (ESV)

As for these four youths, God gave them learning and skill in all literature and wisdom, and Daniel had understanding in all visions and dreams.

I enjoy a good comic book movie like the *Avengers* or *Captain America*. In these movies, it is clear who the stars of the story are, usually Robert Downey Jr. as Iron Man or Chris Evans as Captain America. There is no mistaking who has center stage in the film.

Often in life, though, I get confused about who the star truly is.

In Daniel 1, we are greeted with a familiar story of four young men who were chosen by a foreign king to join the ranks of the elite. In order to be part of the chosen few, the Babylonian Empire required that they be men without any physical defect, handsome, showing aptitude for every kind of learning, well informed, competent for understanding and qualified to serve in the king's palace. Wow! I know that list would have disqualified me from serving in the king's palace!

Getting chosen by the Babylonians for this crucial role was like being chosen in the NFL draft, winning *The Voice*, becoming a supermodel and winning *Jeopardy*. These guys had incredible potential and fit what Babylonian society defined as "top tier" people in society. You would think that chapter one is about these amazing young men, but it's not. It's about God.

Daniel clearly conveys that he, along with his companions, would not defile themselves on the king's food and chose to eat nothing but vegetables and drink water for ten days. At the end of that time period, they looked healthier and better nourished than the other young men who ate the royal food. Perhaps this story is about how we should incorporate Daniel's diet into our life (not a bad thing!). But no, it's not about eating vegetables rather than Uno's Pizza. It's about God, and that's the point not only of the book of Daniel but of the entire Bible.

God is always the star of the story.

In chapter one, it is clear that God gave Daniel and his companions favor before the royal officials. It is God who gave them their incredible health, knowledge and understanding. The metaphoric success of Daniel and his companions in a foreign land is about God and His favor.

Our lives must be lived seeking the favor of God who is always the star of the story.

Are you living as if the story of life is about you or as if it is about the Creator and Sustainer of all things?

Father in Heaven, help me to live my life for you and you alone in all circumstances so that all will know you are the center of my life and the star of the story you write through me.

Author: Jason Esposito

Wake Up

Romans 13:11-12 (ESV)

Besides this you know the time, that the hour has come for you to wake from sleep. For salvation is nearer to us now than when we first believed. The night is far gone; the day is at hand. So then let us cast off the works of darkness and put on the armor of light.

I was thirteen when my mom died. It happened suddenly. One day she was here, the next she was gone. If you had asked me about my faith the day before she died, I would have told you that I definitely had a rock solid faith, completely anchored in the truth and hope of Jesus. The day after, I might have just stared at you blankly, wondering how you could still put trust in a God who could ruin a family in this way.

I spent the next nine months just doing everything I thought I should. I went to school, church, acted like a good person. However, on the inside I struggled daily with who God really was. Yeah, I called myself a Christian, a follower of Jesus, but I never prayed, never looked at Scripture, and basically had nothing to do with God.

Then, I went to Village Creek Bible Camp for a week during the summer. God placed me with a counselor who loved on me for the week and just listened to me. At the end of the week, we were talking alone, and she said something to me that I will never forget. In a few bold words, she said, "You need to either choose to follow God or stop calling yourself a Christian. Wake up, and own your faith."

It is amazing how God uses people to say something to you that you desperately need to hear. As I left that conversation, I remember how the Holy Spirit just started pointing out to me all the ways I had just been coasting through my "faith." He brought me to today's verses.

Even before my mom died, I think I was sleeping in my faith. I sort of did the God thing at church and then did not think about Him any other time during the week. I rested on the fact that I did not do anything too terrible, so God would still consider me His child. I was not actively seeking God or His truth. When the time came for my faith to be stretched, it snapped instead of growing because I was never truly anchored in Christ.

Since that day with my counselor, I keep those verses in Romans handy. It is so easy to become lazy in our faith and fall asleep. I pray that He would daily remind me to study Scripture, to pray, and to know God for myself. Only in this way am I able to be completely anchored in my faith in Jesus.

What happens to my faith when I am not awake and actively seeking God?

Jesus: increase my desire to know you. Help me to seek you daily!

Author: Michelle Jenks

Connected to the Anchor

John 15:5 (NIV)

I am the vine; you are the branches. If you remain in me and I in you, you will bear much fruit; apart from me you can do nothing.

I spent more than a few hours while growing up on the shores of Lake Michigan watching boats travel in and out of the various channels from the big lake to smaller lakes where safe and secure marinas could be found. On a sunny July afternoon, a flotilla of boats of all shapes and sizes would pass through these channels near my favorite viewing station on the shore. And I would dare say that each of these boats was equipped with an anchor.

Larger boats would boast hefty anchors. Smaller boats needed smaller, yet no less important, weighted devices. In observing the boats though, I came to realize that the anchors were useless without one additional piece of equipment—a rope or chain.

Think about it! Have you ever seen a useful anchor without a rope or chain connected to the anchor and attached to the boat?

It would seem almost laughable to see a sailor throw a weighty anchor overboard with no rope or chain tethering it to the boat. The anchor would plunge to the depths of the lake, but the boat would keep moving in the winds or the currents. Not only would the boat not remain in place, but the anchor itself would be lost.

Jesus told His followers that it was critical for them to stay connected to Him, to always keep their lives tethered and attached securely to Him. Using an illustration of a fruit-bearing vine, Jesus reminded us that the branches must stay connected to the vine if we are to bear real spiritual fruit. In fact, Jesus said that failure to stay connected with the vine would result in fruitlessness. Anchors must stay connected to boats. Branches must be connected to the vine.

I have found my connection with God works best in a moment by moment conversation with Him. A conversation simply means me listening to God and then responding to Him. It is a back and forth dialogue that keeps me connected with His voice, His direction, and His will. It is a conversation that continues throughout each day, and takes place thousands of times. It is a connection that brings life— the real life of Christ—to my soul. Without this ongoing conversation, my soul would go adrift, untethered to my source of life and my anchor.

When is the last time you had a long conversation with the God who is both good and great, and desires for you to connect with Him?

Whether in a quiet meadow or a crowded street corner, God is always ready to connect with you.

Loving God: keep me connected to You today as we walk and talk together.

Author: Dan Hamil

Unchangeable, almighty Lord,
Our souls upon Thy truth we stay;
Accomplish now Thy faithful word,
And give, O give us all one way! [vi]

CHARLES WESLEY

Unchanging

Malachi 3:6 (NLT)
I am the Lord, and I do not change.

I hate change. I have always hated change. Life events that other personalities might approach with excitement or anticipation leave me feeling afraid and uncertain. I have spent most of my life avoiding these situations at all cost.

Unfortunately for me, many changes in life cannot be avoided. For example, most of us will not live our entire life in one home - God has gifted me with twenty-one in forty-five years! People we love will die. Friends will move away. Graduations, weddings, funerals...they are all a part of normal life, and they all represent a change of some kind.

I am currently in the stage of life in which my own children are graduating high school, moving out, and getting married...and not all in that order! Had I thought ahead at all, I would have bought stock in a tissue company. All of these changes have left me feeling sad, overwhelmed, and more than a bit out of control.

I am so thankful that, while it is true that we live in a constantly changing world, we have access to a never-changing God. Today's verse is my favorite Bible verse. If tomorrow I wake up to an upside down world, I know that my Heavenly Father will remain unchanged. His love for me is a constant. His desire to have a relationship with me need never be in doubt. He is my anchor.

The very nature of an anchor is its stability. When put to work, an anchor provides stability. It is immovable. It is unchanging. How fitting that as believers we can choose to attach our lives to the true anchor-Jesus Christ, who also by His very nature is unchanging.

Does your life sometimes seem out of control? Are you like me, and find change intimidating? If so, I hope that you will find hope in the only unchanging and immovable God. He offers you His love and forgiveness. He desires to be a part of your life and to give you that solid anchor that you need in a sometimes uncertain world.

Heavenly Father, thank you so much for being my anchor. Thank you that when life seems to be changing rapidly around me, that you will never change. Please help me to put my trust in you in ALL circumstances, whether familiar or new.

Author: Dina Hanken

Trusting My Anchor

Isaiah 41:10 (NASB)

Do not fear, for I am with you;
Do not anxiously look about you, for I am your God.
I will strengthen you, surely I will help you,
Surely I will uphold you with My righteous hand.

"The width of the valley is 3 screams long," said my husband, who counted how many times I emptied my lungs as I flew across the valley on the zip line several years ago at Village Creek Bible Camp.

Apparently I was unable to contain my "joy" as I felt my life flashing before my eyes when I jumped off a platform into what seemed like the literal last thing I would do on this earth. Gliding 800 feet across the valley, I should have been happy because I was certain I was going to meet Jesus. But, I didn't meet Him that day. I survived.

When I think about being *anchored*, I am reminded of that day. I was terrified. All I could do was "anxiously look about me." It was a palpable fear and apparently quite humorous to those around me. But, not funny to me. My heart was pounding. Anxiety flooded my entire being. Survival was my only goal. Adrenalin rushed through my body.

Ultimately, it was a matter of trust. It was a matter of trusting I was anchored securely.

Sometimes in life it seems easier to scream as we fly across the valley. We seek out anxious thoughts and camp out there. Maybe it is an internal scream, or maybe we lash out at others in our own response to anxiety or fear. Everyone around us hears it at some level. Our attitudes or our actions or even our words all speak what is inside our hearts.

God doesn't really give us an option here. He just says, "Stop it. Do not fear. Don't go looking for anxious thoughts. Trust me. Anchor yourself to Me. For I am your God. What else do you need? I will help you and uphold you."

We must stay tethered or anchored securely in Him through His Word, even when we fly across the valley, whatever that may be.

If our foundation is in Christ and we are grounded in His Word, we have what we need. His Word is my anchor and sometimes I forget that.

Valleys are no stranger to me. The darkest has been the "valley of the shadow of death." I've lost two babies within an hour of birth, a six year old to cancer, and both of my parents. Everyone has a valley in their story at some point - maybe more than one.

In the quiet of the night or in the harsh reality of the day, He has been faithful. He has strengthened, helped, and upheld me. What a waste of time and energy to "anxiously look about me."

He is My God.

Thank you, Lord, for being my God, for strengthening me, and for upholding me through all of the valleys.

Author: Heidi Jundt

Training for Godliness

I Timothy 4:8 (NIV)

For the training of the body has a limited benefit,
but godliness is beneficial in every way,
since it holds promise for the present life and also for the life to come.

Professional athletes have to be very good at training. I remember watching a workout session of several NFL Pro-Bowl receivers lead by former Viking Chris Carter. It was crazy intense and amazing. I was tired just watching.

One of the pro snocross racers I interviewed once for a clinic told me that he puts in over 5000 laps on a track by the time the season starts every year at the Duluth National, the day after Thanksgiving. Now that is some serious training.

The apostle Paul talks about physical training in today's passage. He tells young Timothy that physical training is good and that there is nothing wrong with it. It is important and has value.

However, Paul drops some serious truth on Timothy and talks about how much more godliness has massive benefits to us both now and on the other side of eternity. Training in godliness is beneficial in every way.

Godliness simply means working hard to make our life – our beliefs, thoughts, and actions – line up with the Creator's way of life. The closer we push our hearts to beat in unison with Christ, the more like God we become.

How would you rate your recent physical training? Poor? Average? Excellent?

How would you rate your "godliness" training recently?

Dear Jesus: I want to follow you more closely and "train" my heart and mind to be in step with your way. I pray that you would help me. I pray that you would teach me. I pray that through your love and grace I would become stronger in my godliness. Thank you, Jesus. I love you, Jesus.

Author: Jake Vanada

A Shelter in the Storm

Psalm 34: 4 (NIV)

I sought the Lord, and He answered me;
He delivered me from all my fears.

It is 3:07 a.m., and I am wide-awake.

This is becoming a nightly ritual. I toss and turn. My thoughts tumble from one concern to another.

I am a high school teacher, so I wonder, "Did I handle that situation or that student in school correctly?"

I think some more, "What issues will my granddaughter with down syndrome face as she grows up?"

And then, "Will my sons find girlfriends who love the Lord?"

I am a pastor's wife, so I worry, "Did I offend the lady in church by what I said or did not say?"

Now it is 4 a.m., and I fret about what is going on in our nation and in our world! I am scared! I think some of these thoughts in the daytime would seem foolish, but in the dark of the night, they all seem overwhelming!

Finally I turn to Jesus with these worries. *Why do I wait so long to turn to Him?!*

I love a song that we sing in church; here is its first verse:

"I have a shelter in the storm when troubles pour upon me. Though fears are rising like a flood, my soul can rest securely. O Jesus, I will hide in You...my place of peace and solace. No trial is deeper than Your love that comforts all my sorrows."[vii]

Jesus is my shelter in the storm that is raging in my soul at 3:07 a.m. Though fears are rising like a flood, my soul can rest securely in Jesus. What a picture! What a truth! So, as I turn to Jesus in the middle of the night, I start to PRAY, PRAY, PRAY.

I review Scripture passages that I have memorized such as: Colossians 3:2: *"Set your minds on things above, not on earthly things."* Colossians 3:15: *"Let the peace of Christ RULE in your hearts, since as members of one body you were called to peace. And be thankful."* I praise the Lord as I recite Psalm 8, *"O Lord, our Lord, how majestic is your name in all the earth."*

Soon, my thoughts are on the LORD and not on my worries, and I have peace and I FALL ASLEEP! Truly I can say, *"I sought the Lord, and He answered me, and He delivered me from all my fears."*

Lord, thank you for being my shelter in the storm when I am worrying about "things" going on in my life. Thank you for delivering me from all my fears!

Author: Joanna Lerud

Renew My Life

Psalm 119:37 (NIV, 1978)
Turn my eyes away from worthless things,
renew my life according to your Word.

I grew up as a Baptist. In my younger days, we were known for "The 7 Don'ts." I remembered being teased because I couldn't go to dances, go to shows (movies), drink, smoke, and – well – other things.

One time my girlfriend, who was not a Baptist, wanted me to go with her to the movie theatre. I decided that would be fun. But actually it was not fun at all.

All I could think of during the movie was, "What if Jesus would come now?"

That might sound silly to you. And it does to me too now. BUT....

I soon realized that it was not that I could not go to movies. What my parents were trying to teach me was from God's word that says, "Turn my eyes away from worthless things." They did not want me watching things that would turn my heart from following Jesus and what He wanted me to do. It was good teaching.

I learned that it was not "don't" do this and "don't" do that. Rather, it was a way of renewing my life to live in His presence.

And what does that mean? God invites us to live with Him – in His space. It is a wonderful place to be. Even in dark times we live in the light. He holds our hand. He walks beside us. He shows us the way. He renews our life each day.

And we can say as David did in Psalm 119:32, "*I run in the path of your commands, for You have set my heart free.*"

Father, how I thank you that we can live with you. We can be your child. I thank you that you lead and guide us as you renew our lives every day. Remind me again today to "Turn my eyes away from worthless things" and renew my life with your Word again today.

Author: Monie Fluth

I need thee every hour, most gracious Lord;
No tender voice like Thine can peace afford.
I need thee, O I need Thee;
Every hour I need thee;
O bless me now, my Savior,
I come to thee. [viii]

ANNIE S. HAWKS

In the Room

Ephesians 6:13 (NIV)

*Therefore put on the full armor of God, so that
when the day of evil comes, you may be able to stand your ground,
and after you have done everything, to stand.*

I was there, in the room, when my mom died.

I was there when her breathing slowed, when her body stopped, when tears fell from her eyes.

I was there when my grandfather spoke, "The Lord gives and the Lord takes away."

I had prayed for healing, for years I'd asked God Almighty in whom every healing power rests to remove my mom's cancer. But there I was in the room standing next to the bed when she died.

I remember sobbing in my old bedroom; I remember sitting on some blankets in the front yard with friends who had come to sit in silence with me.

I remember driving downtown to pick up my brother from the bus stop and on the way back home telling him that our mom was with Jesus. I remember him staring straight ahead and saying, "I know; I felt it." I remember the death tsunami crashing down on me.

I remember learning something very important about God that day - He doesn't take the tsunami away...but I also learned another very important thing about God. I was sure I'd be demolished by that wretched death tsunami as it twisted and boiled over me. And when it hit, it hit hard. I was broken, bruised, and pieces of my life were washed away. But when I opened my eyes, incredibly, I was still standing.

In the today's passage, the Apostle Paul talks about God's equipment, about evil days to come, and about how - after it is all said and done, we are able to stand.

I learned God does not remove the tsunami, but He does stand with us, right there, in the thick of it.

Father God: You are my standing strength when I haven't the strength to stand. I hate how vulnerable and weak I am in this moment; but now, more than ever, I need you. Amen

Author: Benjamin Kelm

A Sinking Feeling Part 1

Hebrews 12:1-2 (ESV)
Therefore, since we are surrounded by so great a cloud of witnesses, let us also lay aside every weight, and sin which clings so closely, and let us run with endurance the race that is set before us, looking to Jesus, the founder and perfecter of our faith, who for the joy that was set before him endured the cross, despising the shame, and is seated at the right hand of the throne of God.

The rain clouds were daunting, and the temperature was dropping in northern Minnesota, but we didn't let that stop us from fishing. My two brothers, my husband, and I took extra measures to dress in many warm layers and rig up some homemade rain gear out of plastic garbage bags.

Not even five minutes into our fishing trip, our boat went from an above water craft to a submarine - literally. As the speed increased, the boat took a nose dive into the water. The frigid water rushed over our feet, and within seconds the entire boat was under water. We experienced a sinking feeling – literally and figuratively!

We found ourselves struggling to catch our breath and stay afloat in the icy cold water. Our thick clothing and plastic bags quickly soaked up the water and began to weigh us down. As the reality of our situation sunk in, we became desperate to locate the lifejackets. It didn't take long for us to realize we had left them in the trunk of the car!

With no floatation devices, our only hope was to cling to the side of the overturned boat. We worked together to try to pull the boat to shore. I felt like my energy would be better used swimming to land to go for help. The guys pleaded with me to let go of some of what I was wearing, but I felt confident I could make it in tennis shoes, a winter jacket, leather gloves, a hat, three shirts, two pairs of pants and two pairs of socks - not to mention the two bags around my feet and the two huge garbage bags wrapped around each leg. After all, I used to be a lifeguard at Village Creek Bible Camp.

I'll never forget when I had the realization that I was drowning – all because I refused to throw off what was holding me back. I liked my shoes and jeans a little too much to let them fall to the bottom of the lake. Now those very things I clung to so tightly were pulling me under.

By some miracle, I made it to shore and lay there like a beached whale. The boys never made *any* progress with the boat because unbeknownst to them, the anchor had fallen to the bottom of the lake and was preventing them from going anywhere. They were hopelessly and needlessly exhausting themselves by pulling on an anchored vessel. Thankfully, another boater rescued them shortly after I finished my senseless swim to shore.

My foolish refusal to let go of what was hindering me nearly cost my life. I was aware of what was holding me back, but sometimes it's not as obvious – like the guys pulling on the anchor stuck on the bottom of the lake.

What has you stuck? Do you feel like you are just barely keeping your head above water? Ask God to reveal any sins that are clinging to you and keeping you from making forward progress. Lay them aside and then start moving as you keep your eyes on Jesus! Oh – and please remember to pack lifejackets the next time you go boating!

Dear Lord, please reveal to me the things that are weighing me down. Enable me with your strength to throw them off and keep them off.

Author: Molly Sanborn

A Sinking Feeling Part 2

Hebrews 12:1-2 (ESV)

I'll never forget the image of those branches extended into the water – almost as though they were reaching out to me. I specifically remember fixing my eyes on that fallen birch tree as I was nearly drowning the day before. The tree had become my finish line, and now, not even 24 hours later, it had become my reference point. That's right – we were back on the same lake, in the same boat, but this time we were wearing lifejackets.

After being rescued the day before, we determined that we would return the next day to recover the items we lost when the boat went down. We hoped to find our fishing poles, the battery, my brother's wallet, and my brother's $600 tooth.

Yes, you read that correctly – Andy's tooth was missing. It hadn't come out when the boat went down, but Andy had actually *taken* it out and put it in his tackle box just moments before we submarined. At this point, you're utterly confused and tempted to skip to the next entry. Let me explain.

My brother had lost his two front teeth in an accident years ago, and had them replaced with fake teeth, one of which had recently become loose. Completely clueless that we were just minutes from going under, Andy had placed his loose tooth in his tackle box to keep it safe. Now his tooth and tackle box were at the bottom of the lake.

While my brothers and I went to treasure hunt, my husband stayed back to "pray" (aka avoid any more near death experiences). We asked God for favor and direction before we left and continued to pray while combing the lake bottom with our extended yard rake and other homemade contraptions. Picture hillbillies, in wet suits, on a boat – one with a toothless grin.

The boys were convinced they had found the spot where we went down, but I had a sinking feeling they were wrong. We were nowhere near the birch tree. Though I adamantly explained my reasoning, they disregarded my suggestion and spent over an hour draining themselves with dives from the boat and blind searches through the muck 12 feet below.

Finally, they agreed to pull up anchor and head to the birch tree. On his first dive to the bottom, Andy came up with the tackle box – still shut tight! Inside, safe and sound, was his tooth! We also recovered a fishing pole, the battery, Andy's wallet and our bag of M&M's! My brothers were apologetic for not listening to me sooner. We nicknamed Andy "Tooth 'n Tackle" and thanked God for that birch tree which had become a very precious point of reference.

In the moments when you are struggling to survive, when you feel like you are treading water, what is *your* point of reference? What orients you? For me, I was focused on that birch tree. It was a fixture that was going nowhere. It drew me out of my distress and also served as a valuable reference point and reminder of what we overcame.

Jesus does that for you. He extends His arms toward you over the rough waters in your life. Will you look to Him? He overcame sin through death on the cross, and great treasure awaits those who focus on Jesus - the most reliable reference point.

Dear Lord, please help me fix my eyes on you always - especially in troubling times. Please direct my heart and focus toward you – the founder and perfecter of my faith.

Author: Molly Sanborn

Our Anchor Transplants Hearts

Matthew 15:18 (ESV)

Do you not see that whatever goes into the mouth passes into the stomach and is expelled? But what comes out of the mouth proceeds from the heart, and this defiles a person.

Garbage In. Garbage Out. (aka G.I.G.O) is an old computer programming term that means whatever commands that you type into your computer is what you will get out - even if that is not what you meant to tell it to do.

Even though I work in information technology, I do not do coding. However, I am well aware of the commands I have told my computer to do. This is especially true when it comes to printing, and not getting what it was that I ordered!

Similarly, in life, we will typically get back whatever we put into life. If we put garbage into our lives, we spew out garbage as well. This garbage is basically anything of this world that we take to an extreme or put to misuse – money, drink, food, etc.

Some of these are essential parts in our lives and are needed in order for us to stay alive. However, there are other items that do not have a place in our lives at all, such as lying, stealing, murder, envy, jealously, impure thoughts, and on and on. Jesus taught that what comes out of our mouths actually comes from our heart. If we have put trash into our minds and lives, then we are defiled.

The Greek for this word defiled means "polluted, stained or contaminated." Literally, the heart has been marred with sin so much that it is not the same.

Think about it from a baking point of view. If you put too much of one ingredient into the bowl, you need to throw out the whole batch and start over.

God has done that for us! He has thrown out the stained and marred heart and replaced it with a new heart! All we need to do is believe that He has died on the cross for us and accept that heart transplant He has given us through His Son. His Son died on the cross and gave us a new heart so that we could live again!

If you have already accepted Christ as your Lord and Savior, what diet are you putting into your mind or heart?

Garbage in; garbage out. The opposite is also true. Which way will we choose today?

Father God: Help me protect my mind and my heart. Help me to only consume things that are needed and to stay away from the trash that is around me. Give me the heart transplant that is needed today and everyday as I live for you.

Author: Cindy Schwerdtfeger

The Gospel is For All of Life

Ephesians 4:1 (ESV)

I therefore, a prisoner for the Lord, urge you to walk in a manner worthy of the calling to which you have been called ...

I am an avid hiker, and living in Arizona gives me access to many trails and mountains. My hiking also gives me access to long, challenging conversations with God, and I do not hesitate to take advantage.

About 15 years ago, while not new to ministry, I was new to being the lead pastor of a local church. Nothing in seminary or life had prepared me for the kind of scrutiny I had experienced in my first six months in this job. And I was already done. But before officially moving on, I took a half-day to wrestle with God about my decision on an obscure, difficult-to-access trail in the central Arizona mountains.

After a 90-minute ride to the trailhead, I got started and wasted no time aggressively engaging God with a pointed request: "God, this job really stinks, and I am done. Give me one good reason I should not just get a job at UPS where no one will bother me."

I had the rest of the day for God to answer, but He didn't waste any time – unusual for when I am complaining to Him.

Immediately, God spoke Paul's words from today's passage into my spirit, and then an explanation that grounds me to this day: "You're correct, Frank. As a job, pastoring is a mess. And as long as you look at pastoring as a job, you will hate it. What you must understand and remember is that I do not give people jobs. I *call* people. I call people to the Gospel, to serve, and to ministry. And because I have called you, I have also equipped you to walk in a manner worthy of your calling. Ground yourself in the Gospel, not in your capacity and the world's expectations, and you will find the correct perspective to fulfill your calling."

How many of us are so grounded in the world and its values, our idols and our comfort, that we never see the Gospel truly work in our lives and our calling?

The Gospel is not just for salvation but for all of life. The Gospel is foundational to everything we do. It is the power of God for the calling of God. The Gospel does not just get us started, but it anchors us in His love, power, and authority for all of life, so that we might live in a manner worthy of the calling to which we have been called.

Gracious God, thank you for reminding me that life in Your Kingdom is not a job but a calling, and as such you have already equipped me. Your power, love, and authority are what I need more than anything the world can offer, and I thank you that your Son has given me that gift through His life, death, and resurrection.

Author: Frank Switzer

Be still my soul: the Lord is on thy side.
Bear patiently the cross of grief of pain.
Leave to thy God to order and provide;
In every change, He faithful will remain.
Be still my soul: thy best, thy heavenly Friend
Through thorny ways leads to a joyful end. [ix]

KATHARINA A. VON SCHLEGEL

His Hands

Isaiah 35:3 (NLT)

*With this news, strengthen those who have tired hands,
and encourage those who are weak.*

Hanging on my bulletin board above my desk are reminders of things I need to do, pictures of special moments and friends, and a handprint of my grandson Daniel. As I stare at his handprint I am reminded of the fun day that we had with him at "Grandfriends Day" at his elementary school.

I am also reminded of how easily his hand slips into mine when we cross a street, his "thumbs up" to us when he is playing soccer, and the way he casts his Spiderman fishing pole. I love how he makes a fist when showing his "guns" (muscles) as he portrays his super hero of the day - Ironman, Captain America, or the Incredible Hulk. I love the thought that he would like to be my 'superhero'!

I rest in the thoughts, reminiscing, and then think of God's hands. His Word tells me that my name is etched in His hand, and I know that He upholds me with His righteous right hand. It is sweet and comforting to know such great love and strength.

When my days are overwhelming, when I am grieving, or when I am feeling a deep loss, it is good to know that the creator of the universe and everything in it is welcoming me with open hands to step into His care. I am humbled, knowing that through His pierced hands on the cross my sins were placed on Him when I should have been the one to take the punishment.

Many ask, "What is my purpose? What is God's will for my life?"

I think the answer has to do with *hands*. We are called as believers in Jesus Christ to be His extension of love to the world today. We are to care lovingly for the lost and for the needy and to disciple with love and with discernment those in our circle and beyond.

Our hands become an extension of Christ's loving hands as we provide meals, texts, e-mails and as we bind wounds or walk with others on their journeys. We take up our cross daily by "nailing our hands" in selfless acts as an intentional choice to honor and serve the LORD by serving others.

When was the last time you recognized and thanked God for the care and strength He provides in your life? How will your hands become an extension of God's love to others?

Jesus — thank you for the anchor of love you have demonstrated; give me the strength and wisdom to be an extension of your love as I serve others. Open my hands to strengthen those who are tired and weak.

Author: Jane Kramer

The Table

Ephesians 2:4-7 (NLT)

But God is so rich in mercy, and he loved us so much, that even though we were dead because of our sins, he gave us life when he raised Christ from the dead. (It is only by God's grace that you have been saved!) For he raised us from the dead along with Christ and seated us with him in the heavenly realms because we are united with Christ. So God can point to us in all future ages as examples of the incredible wealth of his grace and kindness toward us, as shown in all he has done for us who are united with Christ Jesus.

I was invited to a party, not just any party but a gala. It was the kind of event that has photographers, long gowns, red carpets and family jewels proudly on display.

The evening was delightful. Held in an sparkling ballroom, the menu consisted of delicacies like crab meat served over chilled asparagus with grapefruit and a balsamic reduction.

Glasses clinked and candles flickered. The wine was delicious and plentiful. The main course was similarly scrumptious, with the expected-excellent cut of filet-mignon followed by a bourbon-soaked bread pudding. There was no fear of running out of food. There was no anxiety that there would not be room.

Each guest had a place. Each guest was gladly received. There were even extra places available so that no one would be without a seat.

But I was an imposter. My dress was gleefully snatched from the clearance rack paired with my favorite heels from Target and my roommate's earrings.

There was no reason I should be at this party. I was invited by no action of my own. My hosts understood I could offer them nothing of value. I could not even begin to pay for my own seat.

The hosts invited me to the banquet because their child said that I had worth. Their son said that my presence would bring joy to him. Because their son vouched for us, we were welcome. Because of their son, we were invited and escorted to the best seats.

This is grace. We are given what we do not deserve. The price can never be repaid. This is what grace is. And this what we have been given.

Come, there's room at the table.

God: Open my eyes so that I can see those around me. Help me to have courage to invite others to experience You and your Son. Amen.

Author: Bri Turner

Being on God's Team

Hebrews 12:1-3 (NIV)

Therefore, since we are surrounded by such a great cloud of witnesses, let us throw off everything that hinders and the sin that so easily entangles, and let us run with perseverance the race marked out for us. Let us fix our eyes on Jesus, the author and perfector of our faith, Who for the JOY set before him endured the cross scorning its shame, and sat down at the right hand of the throne of God. Consider him who endured such opposition from sinful men so that you will not grow weary and lose heart.

A few years ago I had the honor of spending some time at *Joe Gibbs Racing* and getting to know some of the people on the #20 Home Depot and #18 Interstate Batteries teams. Joe Gibbs is better known as Coach Gibbs; he coached the Washington Redskins (NFL) for 12 seasons. During that time, he led the team to eight playoff appearances, four NFC Championships, and three Super Bowl victories. He was well known for being able to take ordinary players and inspire them to become extraordinary. After leaving the Redskins, he started a NASCAR racing team where he has had numerous victories including two Winston Cup Championships.

I was blown away when I went to his shop. It is a building about the size of a football field and there are over

500 people who make up his "race team." I got to know many of them, and I found that all of them had one thing in common: they were so inspired by Coach Gibbs that they did everything for his pleasure. Then I realized, "Being on a race team is a lot like being on God's team."

As I think about today's verses, I realize that a lot of people are watching my response and how I react when others or circumstances try to push me off the race course. That's why fixing your eyes on Jesus and being anchored really makes a difference.

Imagine a NASCAR race and all those cars pushing for a slot in the next turn and some pushing cars that crash into the wall. It's definitely not always an easy time, and yet Jesus had JOY. What JOY is there that is so inspiring it would motivate Jesus to endure the cross?

Jesus knew the goal was to sit down at the right hand of the throne of God, be obedient, and to hear His Father say, "Well done." He also knew that the only way we would ever have a chance to get into heaven was if He died on the cross for our sins.

Through running the race, even in the hard times, God can help ordinary people become extraordinary if we keep our eyes on Jesus. We can then have hopes of one day hearing, "Well done!"

Father God – As I run the race, I know there will be hard times, but help me stay anchored and keep my eyes fixed on Jesus and remember my purpose, so at the end I will hear, "Well done!"

Author: Steve Ashcroft

One Big Refuge

Psalm 46:1-2a (NASB)
God is our refuge and strength, A very present help in trouble.
Therefore we will not fear...

My son ran away.

Although he is 18 years old and legally can do what he wants, I was shocked. He called school to excuse himself for the day and left a note at home saying he needed time to think and would be back "later." "Later" I realized had a very ambiguous meaning.

Fortunately, I was able to recall a variety of "do not worry" verses from Scripture, and my heart was relatively calm. And for a few hours, I was able to look at the situation with admiration.

Prior to this particular Friday, he had spent many months agonizing over the decision about which college to attend. Although he had been accepted to half a dozen schools, the one that offered the seemingly perfect-fit major only granted him waiting list status. Now what? The tension level in the house had been on high alert. Anxiety to the point of belligerence overflowed anytime post high school life was discussed. How appropriate that he remove himself from his every day responsibilities to seek the Lord for an answer!

My admiration lasted about 12 hours. Then I did what most normal moms would do. I panicked. Where was he?

How would anyone know if he got hurt? Is he really seeking God diligently or just letting his mind wander? What a lack of respect for our relationship; he has always talked through decisions with me!

My frustration continued to mount as one day turned to two, and then two into three. Although Spencer did eventually reveal his location (Village Creek Bible Camp), only receiving four short texts over three days left this mom on the verge of hurt and anger.

Sunday morning, as I was praying for my attitude and Spencer's decision, suddenly the Lord impressed on me that this getaway was as much about *me* trusting the Lord with my son and his spiritual growth, as it was him seeking the Lord for wisdom on his college choice. God not only needs to be his refuge and strength when making these monumental decisions; but God also wants to be *my* refuge and strength as I learn to let go. The fears and doubts that consumed me needed be released to God as I waited for Him to direct Spencer in a way that was meaningful to him. Without any more of my input.

As I poured over Scripture reminding me that God is our fortress, our deliverer, our refuge and strength, I felt His protective covering and knew that I could rest in Him. And even though my world will change as Spencer leaves our home, God's control and direction will not. He is a very present help. And I have nothing that I need to fear.

In what areas can you trust the Lord to be your refuge and strength today?

Lord, help me to cast all of my anxieties on You. Your refuge is big enough and your strength is strong enough to hold them all!

Author: Michelle Pearson

Core

Psalm 62:5-8 (NIV)

Find rest, O my soul, in God alone; my hope comes from him. He alone is my rock and my salvation; he is my fortress, I will not be shaken. My salvation and my honor depend on God; he is my mighty rock, my refuge. Trust in him at all times, O people; pour out your hearts to him, for God is our refuge.

Athletes of all kinds know how important core muscles are to peak performance, power, and balance. Every training program out there has a significant component of back, abdomen, hip and chest muscle focus.

I remember a few years back when I was asked to be the camp pastor at the FCA MX camp in Indiana. I brought along a Honda 450 dirt bike to ride during the week. What an awesome week...sharing about Christ and His love, power, and forgiveness...AND riding dirt bikes on a motocross track.

I remember how much the pro mx instructors talked about pinching the bike and using our core muscles to anchor and balance ourselves as we rode through the jumps, corners, and whoops (the little bumps).

It was pretty clear to me that I needed to work on my core to help me become a better dirt bike rider. I looked like a floppy fish barely hanging on to the bike. It was not a very impressive display of skill to say the least.

CORE muscles are important in every sport from dirt

bikes to basketball to golf. Your "CORE" is also important in your life.

We understand CORE when we talk about our physical bodies. In the work I do with athletes, we often times use the physical world to help us understand the spiritual world.

If the CORE is strong in our walk with Christ or our faith, everything else in our life will be in better shape because of it. In the Word of God, "CORE" is often described as your heart. In fact, Jesus tells us that our mouths speak out of what is stored up in our hearts (Luke 6:45).

What is at the core of you? How powerful is your core in Christ?

Dear Jesus help me to be strong at the core of who I am not only psychically but also spiritually. You are my rock, my HOPE and my CORE. I love you Jesus.

Author: Jake Vanada

Nothing in my hands I bring.
Simply to Thy cross I cling;
Naked, come to Thee for dress,
Helpless, look to Thee for grace:
Foul, I to the fountain fly.
Wash me, Savior, or I die. [x]

AUGUSTUS M. TOPLADY

Leaving Your Mark

Matthew 5:16 (ESV)
Let your light so shine before others, that they may see your good works and give glory to your Father who is in heaven.

Florence Miller, a young Michigan farm girl, went to Japan with another young couple to be missionaries. The young couple lasted 4 years, but Flo stayed for 40. One furlough, when I was around nine years old, Ms. Miller came to my home church and introduced us to Japan and her people. She told us about the children in Japan and how they needed someone to tell them about Jesus. She asked us to pray for Japan, her people, as well as pray about GOING to Japan as missionaries!

After language study, Florence started a Bible study for university students in the Christian Education Center, Tsu, Japan, and 59 years later, I taught university students in the same Japanese center; Flo's impact was still being felt – she had left her mark.

In today's reading, we are called 'salt and light.' In fact, Matthew invites us to make a difference, "*Let your light so shine before others, that they may see your good works and give glory to your Father who is in heaven*" (Matthew 5:16).

What does this look like? How does this work? For each of us who follow Christ, it will likely take on a different look and feel. No matter what, though, making a difference is definitely something we are meant to do.

Light is light – it absolutely must shine. It has no choice. If we are light, we must shine. We have no choice.

Flo Miller made a difference in my life. She left her mark on us during her visit to our Vacation Bible School. Her visit and what she shared with me at a young age is why I am a missionary to Japan.

I, too, want to leave a mark – to be a difference maker! I want my light to shine so that others can see, hear, and know the Savior.

Through the light of our testimony and the impact of our deeds of service, people should be able to see evidence of the presence of God in our lives.

Can others see Christ in me? Is Christ reflected by you? What kind of a mark are we leaving?

Let's go and make a difference. The world is hurting and needs the message about Jesus. Who can we tell today?

Light of the World, shine through me! Help me reflect You, today. Please take control of my words. Fill me with Your words of love and grace. May my actions imitate You. Use them to turn some heart toward You, today. I am trusting You to make a difference. Amen.

Author: Carol Potratz

An Uphill Battle

Hebrews 10:24-25 (NLT)

Let us think of ways to motivate one another to acts of love and good works. And let us not neglect our meeting together, as some people do, but encourage one another, especially now that the day of his return is drawing near.

Mile after mile passed as I ran my first half marathon with over 8,000 runners beside me. I had trained for months in hopes that I would be able to finish the 13-mile race on my feet and in a decent time.

The first six miles went by smoothly at a reasonable pace, but then came mile 9.

I had heard about the possibility of "hitting the wall" at around this distance, but what I didn't expect was a mile-long gradual hill coinciding with this tough mile. As I started at the base, the hill looked like it went on forever. My pace slowed.

I started thinking, "Will I make it up the hill? Will the grandma I passed about a mile back catch me again? Will I resort to walking for a bit? Or will I just bow out all together?"

Encouragement was the key in my uphill battle at mile nine. As I hit one intersection, a huge crowd was yelling and cheering me on with what would have normally been annoying cowbells. They spurred me on.

As I ran a little further, I heard music in the distance. A live band rocked their instruments which gave me another boost of adrenaline. And maybe most important, I came across a runner I know fairly well from the city I live in. He caught up with me and said, "Let's go, and let's finish this thing together." He ran stride for stride with me for two miles with short snippets of encouragement. I believe all these things aided me in crossing the finish line strong that day.

Encouragement can help us through tough times. What's your uphill battle right now? Do you sense God challenging you to persevere?

Be on the lookout for encouragement in unlikely places and remember that God promises to be present in whatever situation we're struggling through. God has designed us to be in relationship with others which opens up the door to receive and give encouragement.

Will I receive it and extend it to others this week?

God, thank you for designing me in a way that requires me to rub shoulders and interact with others. In my battles this week, provide your presence, grace and strength to persevere. Bring desperately needed encouragement from others and help me to see how I too can motivate others towards acts of love and good deeds. Amen.

Author: Bryce Roskens

Cucumber Frescas for Jesus

Luke 10:40 (NIV)
But Martha was distracted with much serving.

The most frenetic storms of life are often ones we create for ourselves. I have the ability to take an afternoon of serenity in our home and whip our family into such a frenzy that the bluebirds of life are spun out like chicklets in a blender.

Martha, Martha, Martha.

Luke 10 tells the story of two sisters who approach Christ differently. Martha works, worries and compares. Mary worships.

I imagine this peaceful, perfect setting, where Christ Himself, God in flesh, is sitting in *my* living room. And I, having been blessed with the hospitality gene and a passion for all things Pinterest, am whipping up lemon scones, an endive salad, and cucumber frescas for everyone. I begin with the best of intentions: to serve. My noble intentions impress even me. High five myself!

If I were truly a modern-day Martha, I might snap a few pics to put on Facebook, tag the Savior, and add a status: preparing a light lunch for the King of Kings!

In the story, it is Mary who sits at Christ's feet. In my life, it could be any member of my family sitting as Mary did. They sit while I work. They eat while I cook. They smudge what I have just de-smudged! How. Dare. They.

I fret, stew, fume, and eventually launch into a storm of self-righteousness that is unparalleled in this universe.

"Lord, do you not care that my sister has left me to serve alone? Tell her then to help me" Luke 10:40 (NIV).

Martha. Martha. Martha.

My judgment trumps their worship. My storm thunders over their peace. My sin drowns their joy.

I have brought my cold front into this warm setting. StormTeam10 is tracking my moves and predicting wide-scale damage in our home. Such self-righteousness creates chaos where there had been peace.

This is tough. As I write this modern-day version of Luke 10, I am Martha. I confess that it never occurred to me to be Mary in the scenario above. But oh, how I long to be Mary!

The truth is that if I take the time to be Mary, I will also eventually be Martha. Or at least serve as she serves. One cannot worship The Lord without following our worship by serving Him. Worship leads to service.

However I can be Martha without ever being Mary. Martha can serve, sacrifice and give without ever worshipping. However, such service is not pleasing. Service without worship is an empty offering.

"Mary has chosen what is better." Luke 10:42 (NIV)

Sweet Jesus, show me where I put serving before worshipping, where I have prioritized and idolized work over You. Stop me before I create these storms of self-righteousness and cause me to be anchored in a life of worship.

Author: Sharon Czerwinski

A Promise of Rest

Matthew 11:28 (NIV)

Come to me,
all you who are weary and burdened,
and I will give you rest.

As a college student I often find myself weary and burdened. My week is filled with classes, a part-time job, a few extra-curricular activities, and a good dose of homework. I actually enjoy being busy, but I know sometimes my busyness can cause me to sacrifice my time with God for something else. I also know that this adds to my weariness.

I have reached low points this year where I felt extremely exhausted and defeated. These experiences are not fun. When I was in the middle of them, they seemed very difficult to escape. For me, I reached a point where it might not have been possible for me to escape that defeat...at least not on my own. In my moment of desperation, there was one way out, and that was through Christ.

Matthew 11:28 begins with the command for us to *come* to Christ. God offers rest to those who come to Him. If we have not found rest, it is typically because we have not gone to God to find it.

The statement that is made, "I will give you rest" is a PROMISE! God promises us the rest that we so long for. So how do we come to Him?

When we feel weary, there are three ways that we can come to Him. The first is through prayer and time spent just soaking in God. When we sit and listen to God, we allow for Him to work in us and ultimately allow Him to give us rest.

The second is time spent in the Word of God seeking His truth. Scripture is a significant way that God can speak to us and give us rest.

The third is fellowship with other believers. Our fellow brothers and sisters in Christ are a very tangible way we can encounter Christ's love. It is important for believers to both pour into others on behalf of Christ and to seek out the fellowship of other believers so that we also can be filled up with His love.

In our coming to Christ, we cannot neglect any of these three actions—all three are vital for our spiritual well-being. When we neglect any one of them, we allow ourselves to be overwhelmed by our burdens and weariness.

God offers us rest, but he leaves it up to us to *come*.

Father God: thank you for your goodness and your incredible promise of rest. Help us to prioritize you over the busyness of our lives and to seek you first when we realize we are falling into weariness.

Author: Kyle Lippert

Our Anchor Directs Us

Proverbs 16:9 (NASB)

The mind of man plans his way,
but the Lord directs his steps.

What does He want me to do with my life? What is my purpose? These are questions that I asked when I was a teenager and wondering what I should do when I graduated from high school. Should I go to college and, if so, which college should I attend?

I had prayed many times asking God for His direction and answer to my many questions. However, I kept doing the planning for God and not waiting for His direction. Once I had chosen a college and a direction, I figured I wouldn't need to ask those questions of God anymore. Not true.

As an adult, I find myself asking these same questions as well. Am I am in the right job? Is this where you want me? Should I be somewhere else? *Lord, I really think I should be somewhere else.*

I have continued doing the planning for God since I really like to plan out my days, weeks, and life, in general. If I don't know the plan, I am fearful about what will happen, and I am not at peace.

In order to calm myself, I would make up 'happy endings' to the fearful stories in my mind. One of my biggest fears is my husband dying before me and being alone.   In order to plan things out for God, I would make up a fairytale ending in my mind about who to date and possibly marry because God really wouldn't want me to be alone.   I was helping God plan my life because it made me feel better about the fear regarding things that were and still are out of my control. The planning I was doing in my mind was really my unbelief in how the God of the Universe could be in control of my life. When I realized this, I confessed to my friend about my fairytale endings to my fears. My friend's response was to quit over-planning the future and to leave it to God.

Because of fear, I was planning out my life because I didn't trust God or have enough faith that He was in control of the path He had outlined for me. I have far less irrational thoughts of my husband dying now that I know why I headed off into this fantasy world. I call fear what it is, unbelief, then repent, and keep my thoughts in the present while trusting that God will direct my path to where He wants me to go.

God is a strong anchor who keeps us on the path that He has directed for us. We just need to hold onto the anchor.

Father God: I repent of my unbelief in you, the Almighty God of the Universe! You know the way I should go and will direct my path. Help me to have faith and trust that you will lead me along the path You have planned for me. Thank you for being a strong anchor that keeps me on the path You have directed for me.

Author: Cindy Schwerdtfeger

No storm can shake my inmost calm
While to that Rock I'm clinging.
Since Christ is Lord of heaven and earth,
How can I keep from singing?[xi]

ROBERT LOWRY

Strength in Context

Philippians 4:13 (HCSB)

I am able to do all things through Him who strengthens me.

When I was a teenager, I wanted a tattoo...badly. I crafted it myself with my less-than-impressive artistic skills. It was an ichthys, a Greek symbol otherwise known as a "Jesus fish" (turns out all the cool Christians had one), with an abstract cross inset that resembled two inverted Nike swooshes. Written beneath the fish was the reference "Phil 4:13." Blue would have been my color of choice. I would draw it on nearly all of my school notebooks. Can you see it? So can I.

Like so many contemporary Christians, I was drawn to these well-known words in Scripture. These words held power. These words were inspiring. These words held the secret to a life of victory, success, and glory. These words would serve as my battle cry before a football game or wrestling match. They would set me at ease before a high school chorus or drama performance. Wherever there was a proverbial mountain to climb, Philippians 4:13 would be the banner in my hand and the song on my heart.

At some point in my walk with Jesus, I was encouraged to start reading the words of Scripture in context. "Wait a minute. You mean to tell me that there is a whole book called, 'Philippians?'" Sure enough, it was there. All of it. I felt like Inigo Montoya in *The Princess Bride* had just confronted me saying, "You keeping using that verse. I do not think it means what you think it means."

I was crushed. My life's motto was built on a lie that I had

103

perpetuated myself.

When the apostle Paul penned those words to his first century audience in Philippi, he never could have imagined how our affluent, prosperity-driven culture would misuse the profound truth God was communicating through him. Likely written from the bowels of a Roman prison, Paul invites the Philippian believers to hear his grand secret: *"I know both how to have a little, and I know how to have a lot. In any and all circumstances I have learned the secret of being content—whether well fed or hungry, whether in abundance or in need."* Having spent years in ministry as the recipient of persecution and hardship, Paul exhorts believers with his personal testimony of contentment in the midst of ever-changing circumstance. Jesus was his all-sufficient source of joy; a wellspring of life that would never run dry, no matter how desolate the wasteland Paul found himself in.

I still want Philippians 4:13 to be my life verse. However, today that desire is fueled by very different motivations. Like Paul, I long to be able to say, "Come what may, Jesus Christ is, and forever will be, enough for me. He is my rock and my redeemer, the unchanging one, the same today, tomorrow, and forever. He is my anchor."

Unfortunately, I still haven't gotten that tattoo...*yet*.

Jesus, thank you for being the one true constant in my life. Your faithfulness is visible all around, and your finished work on the cross forever proved the depths of your love for me. Help me to rejoice in you in the midst of sunshine and storms alike. You are enough for me. Amen.

Author: Shane Rothlisberger

He Sees Me!

Genesis 16:13 (NIV)

She gave this name to the LORD who spoke to her:
"You are the God who sees me,"
for she said, "I have now seen the One who sees me."

There are times in life when despite having a crowd around me, I feel utterly alone. I was having one of those days. I was desperately missing my mom who had passed away a few years earlier in a car accident. Although time had softened the intensity and sharpness of that pain, there were still days where grief would sneak up and blindside me. It was like someone had suddenly stuck an ax in my chest, and I was walking around freshly wounded once again.

While I tried to shake it off and get out from under those dark, depressing feelings, there was nothing I could do. Try as I might, I was sad. I was lonely. And I felt overwhelmed. As I went to bed that night, tears streamed down my cheeks and puddled in my ears, and I cried out to my Great God for comfort and hope.

As I slept that night, I dreamt my mom sent me a letter from heaven. In her letter she explained how the Lord had told her I was struggling and missing her so much and asked her to write to encourage me. To this day, I can clearly see her handwriting. She wrote about the wonders of heaven and how much love God has for us.

But what I remember most about her letter was the end. She said, "Live each day with joy, Jeannine. Live it with joy!" When I woke up, I felt like a weight had been lifted off my chest.

Later that day, a friend and I had a Facebook chat during which she said, "Joy is living each day with the assurance of God's provision." What a promise...God will provide! God saw my despair; He saw me! He provided encouragement. He gave me hope! No matter what goes on in our life, knowing He sees me and is there for me in the midst of troubles sustains me.

Life is hard. We often suffer frustrations, losses, hardships, disappointments, and betrayals. Thankfully, when we find ourselves in these difficult circumstances, we can turn to the Lord. He alone is our anchor to sustain us in trying times. He is the God who sees us and we can be assured He will provide for us.

When you find yourself discouraged, what can you do to remember that God is not blind to you and will provide for you? He alone sustains us in any circumstance.

Dear Lord: I thank you that you are the God who sees me. I thank you for the hope you give me that provides an anchor for my soul. Help me to remember, when I feel alone you are always with me.

Author: Jeannine Sawall

Pay Attention to Connections

Hebrews 2:1 (NIV)

We must pay more careful attention, therefore, to what we have heard, so that we do not drift away.

Late last summer the people in our small group gathered together to enjoy a gorgeous afternoon on the U.S.S. Vincent--the salvaged pontoon boat one of our group docks on the Iowa River just above Iowa Falls. After a couple trips up and down this navigable stretch of river, sharing conversation and amazing chocolate chip cookies, we decided to anchor the boat so the little girls could fish. At the captain's direction, a man of action grabbed a pristine anchor from within a mess of yellow nylon rope. While joking with one of my daughters about the possibility of throwing her in, he heaved the anchor away from the boat with a grin.

We all watched the anchor fly out several feet from the boat, splash, and sink out of sight into the greenish-brown river. As we watched, our hearts sank. The anchor, the mess of nylon rope, and our boat were not tied together. We were still drifting with the current but without our lovely anchor. Of course, the man who tossed the anchor felt awful. I felt responsible too because I had suspected everything was not connected but had said nothing. Of course, the captain who purchased the new anchor that was never used suffered some sadness too.

Jesus purchased a marvelous anchor for our lives. The Bible tells the story of Jesus' life, His death on the cross, His resurrection, and His imminent return. The Bible speaks other truths that give us wisdom to live lives of blessing and purpose and to avoid the folly that brings us great harm. We have this wonderful anchor, but Hebrews 2:1 says we have to pay careful attention to secure our lives to that anchor so that we do not drift away. It is easy to hear a message of truth or to read a great truth but then not connect that truth to our life. When this happens, we keep drifting with the currents of culture instead of living securely anchored to God.

Besides making our own connection, when we see others tossing away the truths of the Bible, we cannot sit quietly and ignore our responsibility to let them know. We are on this boat together.

Reflect on Bible truths you have heard or read recently. Write down ways to tie those truths to your life. Consider sharing your plans with a trusted friend. Ask how he or she is applying Bible truth to his or her life. A good anchor only helps when we stay securely connected.

Lord, help me to pay more careful attention to the truths you are trying to teach me and to firmly connect them to the life I am leading.

Author: Harrison Lippert

So That

II Timothy 3: 16, 17 (NIV)

All Scripture is God-breathed and is useful for teaching, rebuking, correcting, and training in righteousness, so that [we] may be thoroughly equipped for every good work.

The Bible is always part of our time at Village Creek Bible Camp. It is the reason there is such a place as VCBC. It is not VCC (Village Creek Camp); it is Village Creek **BIBLE** Camp.

God knew what He wanted to tell us. He gave the words to 40 different writers throughout the books of the entire Bible. Through those writers, we have God's message to us in many different types and styles of writing. It comes to us in narrative story, poetry, history, allegory, and many other genres.

I went to camp as a junior and high school camper. I returned later to serve as counselor. Over my adult life, I have attended many retreats, family camps, reunions, and in later years "Young at Heart" camp. All of this was exciting, but most thrilling now is to go there to serve by teaching God's Word to junior (elementary school aged) campers.

God's Word is amazing. It teaches us how to live the abundant life. And sometimes it rebukes us when we are going the wrong way. This might sound negative, but God doesn't use it that way. He says something like, "don't go that way; it is harmful for you." And if we do not listen, He then corrects and says something like "this way is better" and He trains us in that way – "*I know the plans I have for you*" (Jeremiah 29:11).

And all of that is **SO THAT** we will be equipped for every good work He has for us to do. And what a joy it is to be in His plan.

It was at Village Creek Bible Camp that my boyfriend and now my husband, Jerry, and I would stand hand in hand around the fireside each year and say, "I'll go where you want us to go." And His plan for us was the best. He led Jerry into medicine and me into teaching. He then said take that training to Cameroon where we lived for many years.

What a joy to be in His plan!

Father, your Word is so full of everything that we need. Remind us to meditate each day SO THAT we will be thoroughly equipped for every good work that you have for us to do. And thank you that when we do that you fill our lives with a peace and contentment that comes only from you.

Author: Monie Fluth

Our Identity is in Our Anchor

2 Corinthians 6:16-17 (ESV)

From now on, therefore, we regard no one according to the flesh. Even though we once regarded Christ according to the flesh, we regard him thus no longer. Therefore, if anyone is in Christ, he is a new creation. The old has passed away; behold, the new has come.

The first thing that comes to my mind when thinking about what it means to be "anchored" in the Christian life, is the anchor we as believers have as a result of our identity. Today's passage could be called Paul's opus, a large artistic work, on the believer's eternal position! Here we have the apostle reminding the people of Corinth of where a Christian's identity truly lies - not in the flesh - but in Christ. Paul wrote this as a reminder that it was Christ, not earthly labels, that defined them.

Today, these are truths we have heard a million times, especially verse seventeen. You may even have it on a t-shirt. It is easy to take these words passively, to see them as nothing more than a cliché. Just as God wanted the people of Corinth to know that Christ was their definition, He also wants us to know this today.

As believers we often allow worldly labels to bind us instead of letting our identity in Christ define us. Labels enter our lives because we either forget or we become temporarily unconvinced of the reality of the Biblical position. We say that Christ is in us, but how often do we actually think on, believe in, and apply that truth?! By being intentional about believing in our position in Christ, we will be less susceptible to lies.

I struggle with mental illness, likely "bipolar." Most days I forget that I struggle with bipolar disorder, but then the symptoms return which reminds me of my affliction all over again. Despite the bad that has come from having this disorder, I see all the good ways God has used it as I get older. Maybe I am becoming "one of those people" who makes everything a spiritual thing, but He does get me through this. I know that. It is not just a ritual. I take medication which helps in the process, but I still have to see myself as God sees me, which is in Christ, not by my flesh's lies. Being a believer does not always take away depression, but it does help when dealing with it.

There are times when we may feel sad and beaten, but the reality is we cannot be defeated. I know that, while the disorder might influence what I do, it does not define who I am. Part of being anchored means embracing and believing in our Christ-given definition, not seeing ourselves in our old fleshly condition.

Father God: thank you for working in all of our trials. Thank you for the work you do in me and through me as I hold firmly to the truths that you love me, you define me, and you redeem me.

Author: Christopher Cantrell

All praise to Thee, who safe has kept
And hast refreshed me while I slept
Grant, Lord, when I from death shall wake
I may of endless light partake. [xii]

THOMAS KEN

A Neon Sign?

Matthew 28:19-20 (NLT)

Therefore, go and make disciples of all the nations, baptizing them in the name of the Father and the Son and the Holy Spirit. Teach these new disciples to obey all the commands I have given you. And be sure of this: I am with you always, even to the end of the age.

So, what are you going to do with your life? Hint - Jeremiah 29:11 probably isn't the answer. While this question pops up in many seasons of life, it seems to really start gaining steam sometime around your junior year of high school. It starts out as, "Where am I going to college?" This slowly but surely leads to other questions like, "What career should I have?" or "Where should I live?" This question eventually seems to be a drum that thuds loudly in the background of the soundtrack of life, growing in volume with each successive year.

People try to be helpful. They give you Dr. Seuss books and plaques emblazoned with Jeremiah 29:11, *"For I know the plans I have for you..."*

Great. So, you ask God, *"What am I going to do with my life?"*

If you're anything like me, you hope to receive a plan, complete with a detailed path specifying your college, major, spouse's name, children's names, and any/all bad things that will happen listed on a tasteful neon sign. You tell God He'll get bonus points if it happens while you're in a chapel session on Friday night. But in my experience...that's not usually how God works. I've thought I was going to be an opera singer, drama teacher, children's minister, public affairs consultant, and a lobbyist. I'm currently, for this time in my life, a lawyer/fundraiser/amateur ESL teacher and baker.

We're not the first people to struggle with this question. It's been going on for MILLENIA. Abraham didn't know. God told him he was going to be the father of a nation. One problem--Abraham was old and childless. God didn't give him the details: God just gave him a direction.

While Jeremiah 29:11 is helpful to remember, sometimes it's better to rest in the knowledge that God knows and that He has already given us the directions. In fact, He gave them to us in big red letters (not quite neon, though) through today's verses.

Go. Make disciples. Baptize. Teach. Know that God is with you.

So, if you're looking for a neon sign, it might take a while for you to find it. But we can look to the words that Jesus said, the ones where He told us what we should do with our lives. The minute details of who, how, where, and what can be answered later. We know the when (right now!) and the why (because He said so). Go.

Gracious God: give us the assurance today that we do not need to know the details because you have given us the commands. Help us to focus on the now while resting in the knowledge that you know our tomorrows.

Author: Bri Turner

Never Alone

Psalm 34:18 (ESV)
*The LORD is near to the brokenhearted
and saves the crushed in spirit.*

Angie and I were married in 1982. With three more years of seminary education ahead of me, we decided to wait before having a family. After graduation, I accepted a call to serve as pastor of Forest Park Baptist Church in Chicago. We moved in December of 1985, and my ministry began on January 1, 1986.

Once situated, we were looking forward to beginning our family. Our lives do not always go according to our plans. Months turned into years. No children! We consulted with specialists with little result. In 1990, we found out that Angie had an ectopic pregnancy and needed emergency surgery. This greatly diminished our ability to have children.

We were brokenhearted. There were many tears. Other couples were conceiving, but we were not. Well-intended comments, meant to encourage, often had the opposite effect. We prayed and fasted, but it seemed that perhaps God did not have children in our future.

It has been my practice to pray while walking in our church sanctuary. One day, as I was praying about our infertility, (I remember the exact spot underneath the balcony), I heard the quiet voice of the Lord whisper, "David, it will be okay." That is all I remember. But it was very clear. This word from the Lord gave me confidence that somehow all would be well, whether we had children or not. About a year later, we learned that Angie was pregnant with our oldest son who was born in October of 1991.

Everyone knows what it is to be brokenhearted and crushed in spirit at various points in life. *"Man is born to trouble as surely as sparks fly upward"* (Job 5:7, NIV). If our lives are anchored in God through Jesus Christ, we can be certain that God is near. Because He is a good God, we can be certain that He has only good in store for us. He is working all things together for good (Romans 8:28), for our good, and for His glory.

The lyrics of an old Gospel song, "God Leads Us Along," provide great encouragement while we wrestle with our circumstances:

> *God leads His dear children along.*
> *Some through the waters, some through the flood,*
> *Some through the fire, but all through the blood;*
> *Some through great sorrow, but God gives a song,*
> *In the night season and all the day long.*[xiii]

Are you brokenhearted and crushed in spirit? Do you feel that God and His love are far removed from you? Embrace the truth found in Psalm 34:18. The Lord is near to you regardless of the outcome of your situation or how it feels. The Lord delivers the crushed in spirit. He will deliver you.

Gracious Father, my heart is broken. My spirit is crushed. I cry to you and ask you take my broken heart and heal it. Deliver me according to your loving kindness. May Christ be exalted in my body whether in life or death. I rest in your presence. Amen.

Author: David Steinhart

Our Anchor Frees Us

Galatians 5:1 (ESV)

For freedom Christ has set us free;
stand firm therefore,
and do not submit again to a yoke of slavery.

My birthday falls on the opening fishing weekend in Minnesota. Because my dad loved to fish, we often celebrated my birthday with a family fishing trip. We would awake early in the morning, drag night crawlers, leeches, and minnows along with fishing poles and snacks into the boat, and motor out into the open water.

When the fish-finding machines told my dad that we had found a good spot, he would stop the boat so that we could plop our poles into the water. Often, my dad would drop an anchor to the bottom of the lake to hold us securely in the center of the good fishing spot. We were free to fish without worry of drifting into weeds, rocks, or driftwood as it held us firmly in place.

As a child, I thought of this anchor as something that held us back. What if there were more fish to the east or to the west? What was wrong with drifting this way or that way? As an adult who has since taken her own children fishing, I have discovered that the anchor is a powerful and freeing device.

The anchor holds the boat in place so that we are free to fish without worry of drifting away from the central spot where we want to be. We are not submitting to the whim and fancy of waves, and we are not finding ourselves pushed into danger.

According to today's verses, Christ freed us to be free. However, we so often put back on the yoke of slavery by walking away from God's commands. We actually choose slavery to our own desires over freedom that comes from obedience to God, who freed us through Christ's sacrifice.

It seems upside down to think that an anchor holding us in place frees us, but it actually keeps us from being slaves to our own desires and interests. The anchor keeps us safe. In that safety, we are free.

When we stand firmly on the anchor that God is for us, we are free to do all the good that He has prepared for us to do and to experience. Rather than drifting against the rocks, we are safe in His care.

Father God: thank you for freeing me so that I can be free from sin. Thank you for being the anchor through all of my days and for providing a place for me to stand firmly. Keep me safe when I want to drift away from you.

Author: Stacy Bender

I Am Not Alone!

Hebrews 12:1-2 (NIV)

Therefore, since we are surrounded by such a great cloud of witnesses, let us throw off everything that hinders and the sin that so easily entangles. And let us run with perseverance the race marked out for us, fixing our eyes on Jesus, the pioneer and perfecter of faith. For the joy set before him he endured the cross, scorning its shame, and sat down at the right hand of the throne of God.

I have had plenty of times throughout my life when I have felt like I am alone. In high school, friends chose to leave me out because I might "ruin their fun." There have been other times throughout my life when I have stood up for what I knew to be true, but there was no one to encourage me.

When I have had seasons of feeling alone, the truth found in the Bible that tells me that I am not alone has helped to anchor me. In addition, I know many who have faithfully walked with God before me, there are many who are walking faithfully with Him now - all over the world, and God is raising up a next generation of faithful believers. It is so encouraging. Jesus is worth following, and I am not the only one.

As the co-director at Village Creek Bible Camp, I find it exciting when the camp is full. I love to look around at campers from other states, and to see the great variety of staff that have come to serve. I have attended conferences in stadiums where there are thousands of people, packed concerts when they are singing praises to Jesus, a prayer rally at the State Capitol steps where there was standing room only, and events at the school flagpole with a dozen others to pray with other classmates. I am not alone, I can see it, and I know that.

When the author of Hebrews in chapter 12 talks about a great cloud of witnesses, he is referring to the heroes of the past (many listed in Chapter 11 of Hebrews), but I like to add all the amazing role models and followers of Jesus who inspire me now. They include camp staff from each summer, campers of all ages, family and friends, athletes, music artists, authors of books that encourage me, and even all the people who have helped write this devotional. They help me to throw off everything that hinders and the sin that so easily entangles and to run with perseverance, fixing my eyes on Jesus! They encourage me to keep on keeping on.

Take time to make a list of 10 great role models in your life who encourage you, and if you don't have any - start looking for them - they are out there. You are not alone.

Heavenly Father: thank you for creating us to be in community with you, for filling us when we are lonely, and for giving us others in the past, in the present, and in the future who will walk with us on our faith journey. Thank you so much for the truth that I am not alone.

Author: Camie Treptau

Not A Wish

Romans 5:1-5 (NIV)

Therefore, since we have been justified through faith, we have peace with God through our Lord Jesus Christ, through whom we have gained access by faith into this grace in which we now stand. And we rejoice in the hope of the glory of God...And hope does not disappoint us, because God has poured out his love into our hearts by the Holy Spirit, whom he has given us.

My non-scientific observation is that most math students fall into one of two categories--they either love algebra and hate geometry or vice versa. Most people I've run into have a definite preference for one or the other but not both. I was more of an algebra girl in high school but I found something oddly satisfying and comforting about geometric proofs. The *if-then* statements led to a *therefore*...a logical outcome.

As I read this passage in Romans, it reminds me of those geometric proofs. Paul is leading us through a logical progression to a certain outcome. By faith...through grace...therefore hope. Paul has a way with words, doesn't he? He manages to summarize the amazing message of the Gospel in a few words. It's not an easy message...it's not a rallying cry....instead it promises things like suffering and encourages us to persevere...but it ends at hope.

The problem is that we sometimes miss the great truth that anchors these statements because of how we use the word hope. I hope I get a good schedule this semester...I hope my team wins...I hope we have meatloaf for dinner... We use the word *hope* interchangeably with the word *wish*. The hope Paul is talking about is not a wish. It is an expected outcome. We are to rejoice in the hope of the glory of God—that great hope that one day all things will be made right and God's kingdom will reign. The hope that Paul talks about is something we can anchor our lives to. It's the culmination of the Gospel. God has made a way for us to be reconciled to Him, and He has given us the Holy Spirit, God Himself, as our helper. That hope stands regardless of what comes our way.

I want to anchor my life to these verses. I want to cling to certain hope - not a wish. These verses are special to my husband and me. They are on our daughter's gravestone. They remind us that by faith we can have peace with God. He gives us grace and that provides us with an amazing hope that does not depend on the sunny skies or the storms in our life. Instead, it is a certain expectation that one day all things will be made right.

Maybe you are in a good season, a season where there is no suffering in sight. Maybe you feel like suffering is where you have been stuck for a long time.

Regardless of your circumstance, take heart! We know the end of the story! The battle was already won by Christ on the cross. One day, when He returns, the old will pass away, and the new will come. Cling to that hope, that anchor, for your life today and live in that hope for your future! It is the beautiful "now" and "not yet" of today's passage. Hope for today. Hope for tomorrow.

Dear Father, thank you for the amazing hope we have in you and the certainty that in the end all will be made right. We will be with you forever. Thank you that, as we wait, you wait with us. Amen.

Author: Jen Woyke

Daily Prayer Guide for Summer Camps

As mentioned in the introduction, the inspiration for this devotional guide comes from the summer camp theme of Village Creek Bible Camp. Because it is one of many Bible camps around the world, we wanted to provide readers with a way to daily pray for any camp with which they are affiliated.

Sunday: Pray that the campers who arrive today, and the staff who are working, would be renewed and refreshed by God's Word as it is read and proclaimed throughout the week. Ask God to prepare their hearts so that they would want to know Christ more and more.

Monday: Pray that staff and counselors would be anchored to the truth of the Gospel. Pray that they would be able to communicate that truth in a clear and compelling way to campers.

Tuesday: Pray that the staff, counselors, and campers would see God at work in their lives. Ask Him to open their hearts so that they can see their future in Christ regardless of what their current circumstances may be.

Wednesday: Pray that God would bring to light areas of sin for campers and staff alike. Pray that He would work in mighty ways to make all things new in their lives.

Thursday: Pray for campers as they begin to think about returning home. Pray that they would have strength and courage to take the lessons they are learning home with them and that they would live for Christ in their homes, their schools, and their communities.

Friday: Pray for the staff across the camp, many of whom serve in the background. Ask that God be their sufficiency and joy today. Ask God to remind them that they are called to this place and time for a purpose.

Saturday: Pray for relaxation for the amazing staff who work week after week ministering to campers. Pray that God in His mighty power would bolster their excitement, patience, and energy for the next round of campers.

About the Contributors

Dan Andrews is a pastor and father of five. He pastors in small town Iowa and has had the privilege of speaking at Village Creek many times over the past two decades. He is thankful for the camp's beautiful valley to see God's creation and hear God's Word.

Courtney Aronson is a senior at the University of Wisconsin-La Crosse. She is studying interpersonal communication and Spanish and loves to serve at both Village Creek Bible Camp (VCBC) and Side By Side ministries in the Twin Cities. She writes a blog that can be found at beatsforone.blogspot.com.

Gela Sawall Ashcroft is a musician, bookkeeper, computer programmer, wife, and a mother of four. She's been to Village Creek Bible Camp since it opened and loves to lead music with her family at retreats and visit as often as possible!

Steve Ashcroft is a Master Electrician, writer, husband, and Father of four. He's been a guest speaker and lead worship at retreats at Village Creek Bible Camp over the past 25 years, but his major investment at Village Creek was putting miles and miles of wire in the Dining Hall!

Kerry L. Bender is a preacher, teacher, and speaker. He is the Director of the Christian Leadership Center and a campus chaplain at the University of Mary in Bismarck, ND. In addition, he is the Teaching Pastor at Bismarck Baptist Church. His interests include the theology of proclamation, bringing the academy into the local church, issues involving science and theology, and ecumenical dialogue. He and his wife (Stacy) are empty-nesters with two adult children, one daughter and one son.

Stacy Bender is a pastor's wife, an administrator at an online high school in Minnesota, and an adjunct professor at the University of Mary in Bismarck, ND. She writes (off and on) at a blog: slowingtheracingmind.wordpress.com. She has attended Village Creek for over a decade and is thankful for the impact it has had on her entire family.

Christopher Cantrell holds a BA in Biblical Studies and Theology from Emmaus Bible College in Dubuque, IA. He is a teacher, speaker, reader, writer, and wanna-be theologian. Curious about anything

Christianity or culture, Chris strives to live in a manner that abandons the Christian lifestyle and embraces the Christian life. Follow him: www.chronologyofchris.wordpress.com.

Jonathan Chavalas is a junior at UW-La Crosse where he studies political science and communications. He has a deep love of studying the Bible and discussing it with others.

Sharon Czerwinski: passionate pursuer of all things Jesus • wife to Mr. Awesome • mother of two comedians • teacher • communicator • writer • sometimes thinker • mathematically impaired • musically challenged • exhausted by change • seeking rest • content with M&Ms • rabid fan of VCBC and all things camp!

Abigail Dodds is a stay home wife and mama. She's married to Tom and spends her time caring for their 5 kiddos, tackling Mount St. Laundry, getting to know God in His Word, and occasionally blogging at hopeandstay.com.

Jason Esposito is a husband, father of four and lead pastor at Crossway Church. He received his MRE at Trinity International University and Doctor of Ministry at Bethel University. VCBC is one of his favorite places for the past twenty years. You can listen to Jason's sermons at crosswayc.org.

Monie Fluth has been married to her best friend and sweetheart, whom she met at VCBC, for 60 years. She and Jerry have five children, 14 grandchildren, and five great-grandchildren. Together, they served as full-time missionaries to Cameroon for 25 years and have returned on several short-term trips. Monie desires for all to know God and His Word in a life-changing way and teaches at VCBC junior camps whenever she is able.

Dan Hamil is the Executive Director (Interim) of the North American Baptist Conference of Churches. He lives in Rocklin, California, is married to Rhonda, and has two kids who are both studying at universities in the Midwest. For leisure, he enjoys hiking in the Tahoe National Forest.

Dina Hanken is a wife and mom of five kids. She and her husband TJ have spent the past twenty four years in full time Christian ministry. She became acquainted with Village Creek Bible camp in 2000 and loves attending retreats and camps in the valley at every possible opportunity. Dina appreciate VCBC because of the teaching and training up of her children who have served on summer staff.

Lori Hetteen is an artist, illustrator, tulip lover, and black coffee drinker. She accepted Christ in the outdoor chapel at Village Creek Bible Camp as a fifth grader, later got her first job there, and met the guy she would marry in the activity center. VCBC has her heart. She lives in Minneapolis with her husband and four children. You can find her work at www.cherrysparrow.etsy.com.

Michelle Jenks worked for ten years on staff at her church with the youth group. Now she is a stay at home mom just trying to keep up with her two active boys. She still volunteers with the youth and loves teaching and helping others to see the truth in God's Word.

Heidi Jundt is a wife and mom who knows the God of comfort intimately after much loss. She celebrates the God of the ridiculous as she mothers their college son and three adopted children from China. A little bit of crazy covered in a lot of love.

Benjamin Kelm is an artist, pastor, and candy snob who spends his days helping the young adult heart. He says things like "fascinating" and "let's go questing." When not shamelessly extroverting on everyone in the room he's been known to quietly express himself with wool vests, office decor, and Instagram.

Jane Kramer is a speaker, teacher, and Bible study leader for women's retreats and events. She loves to unfold scriptures in a way that captures women's hearts and encourages them in good times and bad. There is nothing more exciting to her than when women are restored and renewed in the Lord. Connect with her by email: jkramer@heartofiowa.net.

Debbi Ladwig is on full-time staff at VCBC. She is mother to two adult daughters and their husbands and "Io-Gram" to five grandchildren. While her primary responsibility at camp is to prepare hearty meals you'll want to come back for, she also loves to serve up solid Biblical teaching in both oral and written form.

Joanna Lerud is a mom of four, a grandma of three (soon to be five!), a high school teacher, and a pastor's wife. Her first visit to VCBC was in 1976 when she spent a month at camp training for God's Volunteers/New Day. VCBC family camp is her family's favorite vacation.

Harrison Lippert lives in Steamboat Rock, Iowa with his wife Pam and the youngest four of eight children. Harrison serves Steamboat Rock Baptist Church. VCBC has blessed them in many ways the last 12 years and for 8 consecutive summers one, two, or three Lipperts have served on staff.

Kyle Lippert is a Music Education student at Concordia College in Moorhead, MN. He has attended Village Creek as a camper since 2004 and joined the staff in 2010. This summer he will be counseling and leading worship. Kyle loves to write music that you can access through Facebook.com/kyle.lippert.music.

Michelle Pearson is a wife, former high school teacher, and mother of four children on earth. She loves leading Bible studies, chatting on a run, and taking photos – all in between carpooling to soccer fields and basketball gyms. Village Creek has been a priority for over 10 years for her whole family.

Carol Potratz had parents who hosted missionaries, traveling evangelists, foreign students, salesmen and hobos. Through these experiences, Carol developed a life objective to know Christ and to make Him known, and God has called her to do that in many ways over the years. She is currently on home assignment after several years in Japan. She pursues and shares with others her interests such as cooking, theater, painting, communication, discipleship, and BIBLE!

Bryce Roskens and his beautiful family live in Iowa. As the youth pastor at Steamboat Rock Baptist Church, he has been pointing teens to Jesus for a decade, which includes bringing students to VCBC on many occasions. He knows the power of "camp" as he gave his life to Jesus at 11 while attending a Christian camp.

Shane Rothlisberger is the family pastor and finance director at Cornerstone Church of Ames, IA. He grew up attending Village Creek as a camper and served as a counselor for a couple of summers. He and his wife, Michelle, live in Ames with their five children. Follow him on Twitter @pastorshaner.

Molly Sanborn is a wife, mom, and speaker. Her life has been forever impacted by Village Creek Bible Camp. She started as a camper, then dishwasher, lifeguard, counselor, and now comes back as a speaker. God wrote Molly and her husband a pretty sweet love story. You can find information about this, her speaking engagements, and more at www.CraigandMolly.com.

Jeannine Sawall is a wife and mother of four boys. She works in property management, writes for FreshStart Devotions (oakwoodfreshstart.blogspot.com), and ministers to those experiencing grief. Jeannine lost her mom 5 1/2 years ago in a car accident and shares openly and honestly about her journey through grief and "the missing."

Cindy Schwerdtfeger is a wife and a mom of two grown kids, a son-in-love, and soon to be daughter-in-love. She is also a grandma of two. Manager of information services by day, Cindy also leads women's Bible studies She is currently attending graduate school for IT Management and enjoys being a student again.

David Steinhart is married to Angie and has two adult sons. He has served as pastor of Forest Park Baptist church in Forest Park, Illinois for the past 30 years. On various occasions he has spoken at the Young At Heart retreats at Village Creek.

Randy Strickland is the worship pastor at New Community Church in Muskogee, Oklahoma. He, his wife Laci, and all four of their awesome kids love Village Creek.

Frank Switzer is the Lead Pastor of Redemption Church Arcadia in Phoenix, Arizona, and an adjunct professor of human communication at Fuller Theological Seminary Arizona and Paradise Valley Community College. Frank, his wife Jackie, and their two daughters (Shelby and Darby) have attended and served at VCBC family camps and retreats for the past 18 years.

Camie Treptau currently works at Village Creek Bible Camp and attended VCBC growing up. There are all sorts of special spots around camp that have special memories, but the outdoor chapel with the creek running near is one of her favorites. At the end of a summer, she makes it a priority to go sit by the creek and list all the blessings from the summer – often she lists campers and staff by name.

Bri Turner is a commercial litigator in Dallas, Texas, and is engaged to Logan. Before defending "the man" and moonlighting as a human rights attorney, she worked at VCBC for five summers (with a week or two here and there during the summers of law school). She enjoys following Jesus on adventures - whether they're in the courtroom, cubicle, or foreign country.

Jake Vanada is a pastor, teacher, speaker, and snocross race chaplin who works with the Fellowship of Christian Athletes in the Minneapolis Area. He is passionate about seeing students and coaches find and follow Jesus. Jake's wife Christy grew up going to Village Creek and Jake has spoken at summer camp and fall and winter retreats many times over the years.

Austin Walker is a follower of Jesus, husband, father of 3, pastor, and youth ministry enthusiast. He loves VCBC because it isn't optional; the love of his life, Calli, had her life completely changed by their ministry. He has a heart for reaching youth for Jesus, and loving their leaders. He is a campus pastor at Embrace Church and is the founder of Youth Leaders Summit (YLSummit.com).

Jen Woyke lives in the Minneapolis area with her husband of 20 years and their three children. She serves in many capacities in the Christian education arena as she is passionate about church history, hymnology, and the Word. Her first trip to Village Creek Bible Camp was over 15 years ago, and she's been going back ever since!

About Village Creek Bible Camp

Since its first family camp over Memorial Day weekend in 1972, Village Creek Bible Camp has offered diverse, year-round programming on its property. Summer camps for young people, family camps, and retreats throughout the year encourage, inspire, and challenge people of all ages in their relationship with God through Jesus Christ.

With something for everyone of every age (horses, adventure-style programming including a zip-line and ropes' course, a lake, hiking trails, crafts, an indoor gymnasium, and more), Village Creek Bible Camp provides quiet times for personal reflection, activities for fellowship and discipleship, and spiritual food from speakers to help those in attendance to find a relationship with God through Jesus Christ or to grow closer and deeper in their existing faith.

All of the contributors to this book have a connection to Village Creek Bible Camp. Many have been campers (child, youth, adult, or family) for several years – some for only a few years while others have been involved for decades. Several have served as staff, speakers, or volunteers. All have a fondness in their heart and a gratitude for the camp and what it has done, is doing, and will do in the lives of children, adults, and families.

For more information about the camp, its programming, and ways for you to contribute to its ministries, please go to the following website: www.villagecreek.net.

End Notes

[i] Owens, Priscilla J (words) and William J. Kirkpatrick (music). "We Have an Anchor." Public Domain. 1882.

[ii] PBS Newshour – April 1, 2015
http://www.pbs.org/newshour/updates/tiny-songbird-flies-transatlantic-nonstop/

[iii] Mote, Edward (words) and William Bradbury (music). "My Hope is Built on Nothing Less." Public Domain. 1836.

[iv] Rippon, John. "How Firm a Foundation." Public Domain. 1787.

[v] Spafford, Horatio (words) and Philip Bliss (music). "It is Well." Public Domain. 1876.

[vi] Wesley, Charles. "Unchangable, Almighty Lord." Public Domain. 1742.

[vii] Cook, Steve, Vicki Cook, and Bob Kauflin. "I Have a Shelter." Lyrics. Come Weary Saints. Sovereign Grace Music, 2010. CD

[viii] Hawks, Annie S (words) and Robert Lowry (music). "I Need Thee Every Hour." Public Doman. 1872

[ix] Von Schlegel, Katharina A. (words) and Jean Sibelius (music). "Be Still My Soul." Public Domain. 1855.

[x] Toplady, Augustus M. "Rock of Ages." Public Domain. 1775.

[xi] Lowry, Robert. "How Can I Keep From Singing?" Public Domain. 1868.

[xii] Ken, Thomas. "Awake, My Soul, and With the Sun." Lyrics. Public Doman. 1674.

[xiii] Young, George A. "God Leads Us Along." Lyrics. Public Domain. 1903.

Made in the USA
Lexington, KY
23 November 2015